Letters
of a C.O. from
Prison

Letters
of a C.O. from
Prison

Timothy W. L. Zimmer

The Judson Press, Valley Forge

LETTERS OF A C.O. FROM PRISON

Excerpts of some of the letters in this volume were
originally edited and published by Arthur Kanegis in
Prism magazine, Spring 1968, at Earlham College, Richmond, Indiana, and are used here by permission.

Standard Book No. 8170-0448-3
Library of Congress Catalog Card No. 73-83735

Printed in the U.S.A.

This book is for Art Kanegis,
who first edited my letters for *Prism;*
for my father,
who did most of the work for the present volume;
and mostly for Toni,
who has helped me in more ways than one.

C. 1

Introduction

THE LETTERS which appear in this book were written by Timothy Zimmer from the Federal Youth Center in Ashland, Kentucky. While a student in Earlham College, Tim decided that he could not, in conscience, retain his II-S deferment. After being reclassified I-A in October, 1966, he mailed his draft card to President Johnson. When his draft board returned it to him, he tore the card into pieces and sent it back to the board. They taped the pieces together and again returned the card to him.

When Tim refused induction into the Armed Forces, he was indicted for violation of the Universal Military Training and Service Act. The draft board placed on record that Tim had notified the board of his unwillingness to cooperate with the Selective Service law and of his opposition to the war in Vietnam, and also that they had not received notice of his class rank status in order to renew his student deferment. At his hearing on April 18, 1967, Tim pleaded *nolo contendere* to the charges, meaning that he would not dispute the facts as presented, but neither would he acknowledge guilt. He also submitted "The Statement to the Court" which has been included in this book. On April 27 Judge David S. Porter sentenced Tim to a term of up to three years in prison, explaining the sentence in the remarks which have also been included in this book.

The letters which follow were addressed to his fiancee Toni Malloy, to his parents Mr. and Mrs. Walter Zimmer, his sister Judy, his brother Richard, and to two of his friends, Arthur Kanegis and Ellie Stern.

Statement to the Court

by Timothy W. L. Zimmer as edited
for publication in *The Earlham
Review,* Summer, 1967

I HAVE REFUSED to be inducted into the armed forces of the United States; I have refused to obey orders issued by my draft board in compliance with a United States Statute; I have refused and shall continue to refuse to associate myself knowingly with the Selective Service System or with the American military establishment.

As a consequence of my actions I face a legal liability of no small moment. I have had to consider the personal and social consequences which my actions may bring upon myself and my family. I have been acutely conscious of the extreme complexity of the issues which are implied by my decision. Any assertions of principle and belief which I have made are not answers to the problem but are only propositions of faith which I hope will help me eventually to solve and resolve the dilemma in which I find myself as a human being.

My decision has not been an easy one to make: I have been called a traitor, a criminal, and a coward, to mention only the more mentionable epithets. My family has had to bear the bewilderment of their friends as well as their own uncertainty and confusion. My friends have asked me "Why?" and I have tried to explain. Some of them have understood; some have accepted the authenticity of my decision without perhaps fully understanding it; some have not understood and have told me so. It has been in these respects a painful process. But by my conscience and my faith in human dignity and freedom, the decision I have made is the most and the least that my conscience will allow.

I believe that the state does not have the right to compel an individual against his will to serve the society in a positively and explicitly defined role. The state may not command the individual to spend a part of his life working at a job which the state has chosen and imposed upon him.

It is the duty of the state and the function of law to define what actions the individual may *not* take with impunity. The state may say what the individual may not do: he may not violate the rights of others, he may not harm the lives or property of others. But beyond this, beyond saying what an individual may *not* do, the state has no right to go further and say what an individual *must* do. Human decency may compel the individual to rescue the drowning child, but the state may not make a law demanding this positive action. A sense of justice may lead one to study and practice law, but the state may not compel a person to become a lawyer. The state may prohibit violence and murder, but it may not compel a person to be violent, to murder. The sense of patriotic obligation may lead one to enlist in an army, but the state may not compel the individual to become a soldier. The sense of social obligation may lead one to devote his efforts to hospital work, but the state may not compel one to become an orderly.

The Selective Service System is a system of conscription, of involuntary service. It violates in principle the freedom of the individual to be, within the legitimate limits of the law, whatever he chooses to be. Paragraph 462 of Title 50, Appendix, of the United States Code is an improper law. It creates an artificial wrong — disobedience of an order — and imposes a penalty for transgression. This law does not command the individual to refrain from violating the rights of others; rather, it commands that you shall not fail to obey; in effect, it says, "You shall obey the order"; and the order is not a law which says "don't," but is a command which says "do." This prerogative does not fall within the province of the right of the state. The state may not say, "do this." When the law commands, "do this proper action rather than another proper action," the law is not proper; the freedom to choose for oneself is always proper. If the law is unjust, the individual has the right by conscience and the duty in principle to try to change, to oppose, and to violate the law. Can the just man abide injustice? Is a man truly just who accedes to injustice?

In view of what I feel is the enormous importance of a human

12

being's right to the freedom of choice, a law which so clearly violates that right and so manifestly destroys that freedom is intolerable. The law must be changed. Until it is eliminated, while it still exists, my only recourse in this situation is to oppose and violate it methodically. This my conscience has demanded and this I have done.

We, as human beings, must preserve the rights and responsibility of conscience. We must be free to choose, to act, and to bear the responsibility for our choices and actions. To restrict an individual's freedom of conscience is to enslave him; to relieve a human being of the responsibility for his actions is to make of him less than a human being. There is no greater right, no higher law than that of conscience. "For conscience doth make men of us all."

Cincinnati, Ohio
April 18, 1967

Judge Porter's Remarks

before passing sentence on
Timothy Zimmer presented orally
in court April 27, 1967

I WILL SAY the first thing I want to say is that the Court recognizes this is the case of a sincere, conscientious objector. There are those who expect the Court in every case involving a violation of the Selective Service Act to upbraid the defendant. I have no intention of doing that in this case.

I was helped in my thinking about this by an article which was authored by General Hershey that appeared in last Sunday's paper in which he said, "Each of us must look within himself to find what is right and wrong — right or wrong. I have a high degree of tolerance for sincere conscientious objectors." He went on in that article to say, however, that: "We compromise whenever we permit some individuals to set limits on their service, and it is only because we are strong that we can afford" what he termed a "luxury of doing that." He indicated if we were smaller we couldn't tolerate it. It would be like — there could be no exceptions, and it would be as if we were in a lifeboat and everybody had to row.

No one has any use for those who are not sincere, and these are what General Hershey called summertime citizens who reserve the right to do nothing and who will not agree that collective action by the United States is necessary. They will not participate in such collective action. He said, and I think he is right as to those, "When the garbage is all collected and the dishes are dried, they shouldn't be around to share in the dividends because they want to be honorary citizens."

While I have said that you are sincere, I think it is ironic that your decision will give aid and comfort to this class of summer-

15

time citizens. It is unfortunate that you will be put in that category by many who may superficially consider your case. I want to make it clear that by nothing that I say to you do I intend to give aid and comfort to the general — those in the general category of summertime citizens, as General Hershey describes it.

I have referred to the report. Nothing appears from the size, but I assure you that it is very complete. I know from that and what your lawyer said that you come from an excellent home. I know that you have been an excellent student, that you have been a good citizen and in every respect except this one matter.

We have a number of letters from students, fellow students, professors, neighbors, from your employer, there may be others; but without exception these paid high tribute to you. I am not sure that any said that they agreed with your position, but all of them said they respected your right to make your own decision. I think they could wish you were a little older before you made that decision. I am sure I do. But these letters were very enlightening, in those and other respects. They have negatived the idea which I thought — well, I wondered about, and that is whether you had some sort of a martyr complex. They negatived this idea.

They have pointed out that you have not been an activist in the peace movement and that you have never been arrogant or other than respectful. To the contrary, I think all of these have pointed out that you are truly conscientious and have a great future. They are hopeful that a committed sentence will not blight that future. And I am sure you won't let it. Probation is just out of the question in these cases. So, you will receive a committed sentence.

I gather that you have arrived at your decision by what seems to me a tortuous route. That may not be accurately descriptive, but your decision is that you cannot cooperate with the system even to the extent of permitting your student status to continue — and that's why you are here so young — much less to apply for CO status. I have no doubt it would have been granted if you had applied for it, and in that event there would have been a number of alternatives to military service which would have been available to you.

Some of the letters urged clemency for you. You have asked none for yourself. The Court is aware as a result that you know that the decision you have made is not only at a risk of a committed sentence, but that in such cases it almost follows as the night the day.

I have tried to come to grips with your position as time allowed and keeping in mind what the Court has to do in passing sentence to see if it made any difference. I must say in this connection it has been frustrating because at no point have I been able to rid myself of the conviction that there is just nothing in this type of case which may be — except a mental condition — which would warrant the Court in granting probation. I do not think I am alone in this. I think that most, if not all, judges feel the same way and that the length of the sentence cannot be less than what your tour of duty in the Army would have been if you had not made this decision and you had been given military service.

My tenure on this bench has been short. We had a few of these cases, none such as yours because most conscientious objectors go the route of applying for that status and accepting hospital or other non-military service. The others have received the same sentence that you are going to get, a period of three years; but they have in most cases had a — all the ones so far have been members of religious sects or their parents have been members of such sects and they have been under the influence of their parents in those cases. The Court can find no reason why they should not serve a period of — their sentence should not be a period of three years.

Your attorney has urged that this will be a tremendous waste to have you out of circulation for that time or such period of time as you come to the point where you are granted parole. I do not think it has to be this way because I am sure wherever you are, in prison or not, you are going to make good use of your talents and that you will try to be a help, either by teaching or some other type of service where you are. I am sure that you intend to write. You don't intend to turn this experience to your profit.

Now, all this leads up to the fact that, no matter where my pursuit of the facts in this case have taken me, I have come back to the conviction that it is necessary in this case to sentence you, and I want you to understand that. I do not think I need to repeat for the record here the basis for your decision; but it is, I believe, understood by the Court. It is not just the Vietnam war. I mean, it is understood that the — to be a larger issue in your mind. It is understood, but I do not agree with it just as many of your friends don't. I know you are respectful of my right to disagree, just as I respect yours.

The sentence of the Court will be, as I have already indicated, that you will be committed to the custody of the Attorney General for a period of three years. Now, this is not done in the spirit of vengeance, not by the Court nor by the law. Neither will this destroy you. Our institutions are modern, and it is not the Court's intention to destroy you. It is not the law's intention to destroy you. But we have to have law. You have made it very clear that you recognize the need for an ordered society and respect for the laws and those whose duties it is to administer the laws, so I want you to understand this because your attorney did think that there was this aspect to it and that a committed sentence might be vengeance, it might have the result of destroying you. I don't view it that way at all.

You have made a lot of people think. I am one of them, but I must tell you that nothing in consideration of this case has shaken my faith in our Government or our leaders who have been selected by democratic process to carry the heavy load that our society has. And particularly, I have refreshed my recollection on the background of the Selective Service Act, and I can tell myself that I can conscientiously enforce this Act. While I may have talked too much already, I have talked to you; but there is a little need to talk to the others whose duty like mine is to enforce this Act; the Probation Department, the FBI, the draft boards, and in the letter accompanying — or in the President's message accompanying the proposed revision to the draft law there was a very clear statement as to its history and the need for it if this country is to survive. It has been on the books since the year before World War II, and it was a very good thing it was on the books a year before Pearl Harbor. There was a world threat that required that it go on the books, and there are a number of things that could be highlighted about that. If you have not read it, I will see that you get it for your reading. I won't continue this longer.

I hope that by holding forth as long as I have — I don't think it has been any ordeal to you. But I wanted you to know that your case has received consideration, and the sentence just wasn't reached in and grabbed out of a bag.

That is all.

Letters of a C.O. from Prison

28th April, 1967

Parents and siblings all —

Greetings from your friendly local convict. Things are going as well as may be expected under the present circumstances. I've been reading (J. S. Mill, T. Hobbes & J. Locke) and getting lots of rest. . . . Today I waded through J. S. Mill's "On Liberty," T. Hobbes' "Of Commonwealth" (from *Leviathan*) and J. Locke's "Essay concerning the True Original, Extent and End of Civil Government." . . . Locke and Hobbes both lived during the seventeenth century, and Mill during the nineteenth. Their particular modes of expression and the perceived conditions on which they, knowingly or in delusion, based their ideas have changed, but the essential problems and dilemmas which they tested and probed are still with us today — what is the legitimate end, what the justifiable means, of civil government? How does one determine, either as general principle or in the context of a particular situation, what are the necessary restrictions to be placed by the society upon the liberty of the individual — to think, to act, to persuade, to dissent? It will take me the rest of my life to frame the question accurately — much less to find any answers. . . .

How are you all? . . . Do you know how Toni is? I don't have enough paper to write her a letter tonight, but give her my gentleness.

I'll need a change of clothing if I am here in Cincinnati for more than another day. If you can get down to see me, bring my book *The Voices of Time* (it was on the chair by my bed).

19

Also a pad of paper if you can. I need my reading glasses (they should be on my desk).

Love and peace,
Tim

Monday, 1 May, 1967

Toni, i love you.

This is Monday — I've been here almost four days. Time in retrospect loses its terror, and the years ahead seem unreal, like a dream neither good nor bad, but neutral — like being itself. Little has changed — it's like moving away from a life's home into a new life; there are people here, and people become friends, and friends become a part of you and change you and make you grow. The only thing that survives from one existential vortex to another is the self; and the self always changes — spontaneously, of its own essence. And the only constant factor in each new environment is man — that glorious creature, the maker of gods and the despoiler of his own integrity — man the selfish, the caring, the loving, the hating, procreator and murderer, knowing and ignorant — man the god and man the devil. Human beings are the least knowable of all creatures — not because they are inherently more complex or inscrutable than other creatures, but because they *must* be known, *must* be understood. Man is the only creature for whom self-knowledge is an absolute precondition for existence. "I think, therefore I am," says Descartes (I think). For man, the converse is true: "I am, therefore I think." It is man's unique attribute; it is his soul. — Enough of this foolishness.

Love, peace
Tim

Toni —

... I am so excited now that I find I may write you. My hand is shaking like the proverbial leaf in a storm. It's been seventeen days since I saw you. ...

Please write — soon, often. ... I read your letter [sent] to the county jail every day. I've memorized it. Your handwriting is beautiful — so fragile, delicate, like you: but so easy, almost inadvertent, like a virtuoso playing Chopin, your words are a keyboard, your meaning is music. I love you.

I want to tell you everything I can about this place where I am, about the people here, about myself, my many selves. They are like — my many selves, that is — like the myriad eyes of (what was his name? Argus?), the sleepless guardian of Juno's geese. "And I am protean in my being. . . ." . . .

But later, later. I shall tell you everything in time, and in time you will know me as only one can know himself.

I don't have the perseverance to keep a diary of my thoughts. Everything that comes to me in sleep and waking, in happiness and in . . . well, there are moments when I miss you most. Everything goes into my letters. . . .

Things are going well for me — there is plenty of vegetable food; the work (I am working in the hospital) is tolerable and sometimes interesting; the library is painfully inadequate, but it should suffice for a few weeks, maybe months. . . .

There are several people here who were sentenced for refusing induction. Most of them are religious objectors — Jehovah's Witnesses — but I have met at least one who shares my own views to a great extent. He reminds me a little bit of Garber, but more intellectual — he was a literature major in college. I manage to see him for a couple of hours every day after the evening meal. . . .

I am staying out of trouble — that's not difficult. People here — the officials — are friendly, even kind. Few of them are gentle, but I can understand that. But gentleness pays — and I have become an inveterately gentle being. Real gentleness means the complete elimination of fear — and perhaps, too, the elimination of fear will lead to gentleness. . . .

Let me know what is happening at Earlham — I love them all, even the crew-cuts and superior smirks and narrow minds. If everybody were like you and me, it would be a nice place, the world; but something would be lost. I need — and you too —

. . . the College Joes and the Susie-Ques of this world. And they need us. Love them and be gentle, love and be gentle — we will conquer humankind. I love you. . . .

Agape and Shalom,
Tim

26 May, 1967
Friday, 5:07 p.m.

Toni, Toni, I love you, Toni.

. . . I have my little ways of getting back at this place: calling meals "dinner," or "lunch," instead of "chow" — being nice to people, being polite, being me, being you — calling the officers "officers," rather than "hacks" — talking to people instead of about them, in front of them rather than behind their backs — liking people rather than hating what they now and then seem to be — liking my work. . . . And, too, I have my little secrets for adapting to this place, to these people: reading, thinking about you, writing, thinking about you and me, talking, thinking about us, thinking, loving you, loving the world in spite of itself, thinking about you, playing basketball, remembering, loving, being gentle, being, being, loving, being, loving. . . .

I am moving up in the world — a rat scurrying from the sewers up into the drainage ditch in the blackest of nights. From humble orderly, lowest of menial workers in a hospital, up, up, from the first floor to the second, up from hands and knees to hind end and head, up from cuts and bruises to severed limbs and appendectomies — in short, from the clinic to the operating room. The work will be better, much better — there is so much more to learn and do and understand and fear and accomplish and be proud of and I love you. Letters are so confusing — please write, confuse me, I love you. . . .

Agape et Shalom,
Tim

22

27 May, 1967
Saturday, 3:24 p.m.

Toni

. . . The other day I was asked to speak with the chaplain. He was supposed to determine my religious beliefs and affiliation. We had a bearable, though slightly tedious, discussion, in which I told him that my beliefs were not classifiably religious and my affiliations were without partiality. I also told him that it was, at any rate, none of his official business. . . .

Agape and Shalom,
Tim

30 May, 1967

Dear Toni —

Today is a holiday. The word, of course, is holy-day, but the day itself is not.

This noon we had a picnic. The sky is a dull gray, the wind is cold and moist. It is, on the whole, the kind of day which should properly cease its early summer foolishness and, in a burst of repentance, veil the earth in generous sunshine and warm breezes. I actually thought for a moment that it might do just that. However, the weather persists, gloomy and unrepentant, and I am driven into the comparative warmth of my quarters. . . .

Love and peace,
Tim

1 June, 1967

Liebe Toni —

Reading your letters disturbs me: you hint yourself in words, give a shorthand account of your soul — bare essentials, incomplete, disconnected, bare essentials. Your letters are like the "connect-the-dots" pictures on the backs of dry cereal packages. They are there, the skimpy outline, rich and unfilled, waiting to be completed, demanding the labor of pencil or crayon to join the dots, to connect the words and fill in the spaces between them with memories and half-memories. And so I do, the pen of mind and memory performs painfully the task of recalling what was best and longs to be good again. It becomes painful sometimes to think of you, as you are now, without me. I have the word-picture and the memory's record, but what do I know of you — are you the same person you were a month ago? How have you changed? . . .

Tim

3 June, 1967

Mon Cherie —

. . . I am in a state of perpetual discomfort here. The tension is quite nearly palpable, as though every other person were "itching for a fight," and were planning to scratch someone to rid himself of the discomfort. I do not "belong" here; so much is clear. But what is to be done? Ah, from what dark corner of my conscience did I drag that query? It is the eternal question of man's condition: I can imagine myself someday residing in perfect ease amidst the utopian fruits of communal labor, relishing the air of friendly, gentle spirits about me, then turning aside with thoughtful mien and asking, quite sincerely, "Ah! But what is to be done?" It's optimists like me that make this world a perfect horror to live in.

Still, I have not answered my question, though I have perhaps suggested that even if the answer were found and quite thoroughly applied in society, I might still be asking, "But what is to be done?" I can imagine, with a slight stretch of my faculties, that God Himself, on the seventh day of the creation, turned discreetly aside from the labor of his days, and queried to the heavens. "Ah! But what is to be done?"

What, indeed. I love you.

Love and peace,
Tim

6 June, 1967

Dearest Toni —

. . . I find myself in a moral dilemma here — I can't possibly explain it completely in this letter, but trust me to understand that human beings can become the agents of extremely ambiguous situations in which it may always be possible to act morally, but not always rightly. The concept of one's "rights" can easily come in conflict with one's feeling of moral duty. If I am wronged, it is my "right" to do wrong against him who has wronged me (an eye for an eye; a tooth for a tooth). If I am wronged, it is my moral duty to behave not as instinctive reaction would dictate, but only as reason and good sense show — for two wrongs do not make a right, and fire added to fire will surely burn the house down. Now, I think I understand this and am willing to accept the consequences of moral action; and so, if the dilemma I have mentioned were principally mine, it would be less a problem. As it is, I am a bystander, guilty as all bystanders are, and the question I have to face is not the simple one of offering right against wrong, or mercy against injustice, but the imponderably more difficult one of weighing mercy against just cause, and morality against "right." . . .

Agape et Shalom,
Tim

6/8 Thursday, p.m.

Dearest Toni of mine —

The daylight lingers long into the evenings now — bids an unwilling, unwilled farewell to the earth, like a lover's pained leave-taking at sunrise. It is as though the sun were slyly and cheerfully befuddling time's conspiracy against our sense of decency, shaking us to a dawn at midnight against the dictatorial regime of the clock. How does one convince himself that time is real? . . .

Agape & Shalom,
Tim

Toni —

. . . Old age is the catalyst which erodes the barriers between generations, preparing the old and the young for the trauma of displacement. The very first poem I ever wrote was about Youth (Thou, Youth, that slips from out my grasp/Throw me not to Age's fearsome clasp . . . etc., etc.). The poem was a lie, of course, I don't remember anything about my youth, and my mother says that I never had it. As to the blissful innocence of childhood, I am so indifferent to the corruption and debasement which accompanies growing to manhood that I hardly note the transition and could care less. Childhood is becoming a thing of the past in our age; one either springs full grown from the womb, innately conscious of the burden of guilt which life bestows, or else he simply never grows up and remains a child for all his life. "Grown men are merely children playing with bigger and more expensive toys."

"And what about you, Sir? Do you believe in a life before death?"

"Cynicism, Sir? Ah! I avoid it like the plague!"

Tim

Meine Liebe —

. . . Being in prison is like being in a state of suspension from life — the sources and causes of one's problems lie behind, and their resolution and outcome lie ahead. The present is a jump of discontinuity — I think they feel that what happens here counts for nothing, that it is like a long sleep during which one solves nothing, decides nothing, resolves nothing; and in the distant morning they will all awake to cope with yesterday's problems, letting tomorrow speak for itself. There are a few who are trying to solve yesterday's problems today, and they are the ones who belong here and may benefit from having been here. The only way to help is to be yourself, to be human, to be gentle — though that is a difficult thing, and the three do not always fall together so easily as they should. . . .

Tim

Judy —

. . . Emil's [a pet dog] death was tragic for you, as though some part of you had been killed. The tragedy lies not in the death itself, but in the survival of you who loved him. Emil's death has meaning only because you loved him and live to remember him. The part of you which died with Emil had to die. You cannot pretend that he is still alive; you cannot pretend that you are just what you were before he died. He is gone and a part of you is gone. But this only matters because most of you is still here — you are alive, thinking, remembering, growing. You cannot stop living because Emil is gone — he still lives in your memory and he will live there as long as you live. Regret his death, certainly; but do not pity yourself on your loss of him. The Emil that was not a part of you, that was distinct from you, a being in himself, has died. You have not lost him, for he was never yours to lose. The Emil that was a part of you — is still, and will always be, a part of you — can never be lost. That Emil will live forever — that is, as long as you live.

Tim

Parents —

Things are better now. I have made an inner rediscovery of myself, of Toni. . . .

I am well. The *Times* started coming the day after you were here. It is a boon.

I need so much to talk with someone, but there is no one here. I miss Dad and Paul Lacey. I miss Toni too, more than anyone else. I could talk with her, listen to her. She says she will be here next weekend. Is everything arranged?

The world is brighter now — not less hostile, but more sustaining — or perhaps it is merely myself.

Love, peace,
Tim

23 July, 1967

Darling Toni —

. . . Time does not exist here — not in any terms comprehensible to the free mind. The smallest unit of time which merits discussion is the month; the week is merely a collection of instants conspiring slowly — too slowly — to gather enough of itself together to become measurable, conceivable. . . .

I cannot conceive of the future — the present so surrounds me, it is like a heavy mist in the morning, blind and so insubstantial. You can gaze directly into the eye of the sun, and it seems no fiercer, no more monstrous than a bright moon. . . .

Love, peace,
Tim

26 July, 1967

Toni Liebe —

. . . Schopenhauer tells a little fable which is instructive, I think. A group of porcupines had gathered together to warm one another against the bitter cold of a winter's night. But it happened that their proximity rendered their quills mutually uncomfortable and so they drew apart. But the cold was bitter and they drew together again only to encounter the previous problem of their quills. Finally, after much trial and error, they agreed on a distance which made the cold bearable and the quills innocuous. This distance they called good sense and propriety.

I love you.
T

28

30 July, 1967

Darling,

. . . I had a good talk with C. We figure that we need about 20,000 people to refuse induction — there must be that many who have thought of it — in order to discombobulate the federal prison system. Ghandi had millions — and they were poor and hungry. Ah, middle-class complacency is the bane of revolution! The Negroes are a hope, but theirs would be a revolution for rights, for justice — it would be (will be?) a violent but righteous revolution. We need a revolution for love, not rights, for gentleness, not justice. We need a revolution for man the human being, not for man the political animal. . . .

Be gentle,
T

Sunday, 8-6-67

Liebste —

. . . Was Prometheus great because of what he did for man or because he defied the undefiable gods in doing it? . . . Let us be magnificent for what we do, not for what we defy. The act — the doing of the impossible — is the strongest refutation of those who proclaim the impossibility of doing it; it is the only refutation, not for proving the impossible to be possible, but for proving that all things are possible.

The weather of my mind is extremely variable these days. I see things which my reason tells me are not possible — and yet they are real. Reason and reality — must the one always be sacrificed to the demands of the other? Rand says that the greatest immorality in man is to refuse to think. She is right. I shall not refuse to think. Ah, but thought and action? I must act as I think, though knowing that the consequences of my actions will affect what I think subsequently. Think/act/think/act/think/act. . . . But when I was a child, it started the other way: act/think/act/ think/act. . . . Somewhere in the process of growing, the cycle skipped a beat: act/think/act/think/think/act/think/act/think. . . . That point was when I ceased to be a child, when my thoughts ceased to be reactions to my acts, and my acts became the expressions of my thoughts. That was the most glorious moment of my life, the moment of my self-discovery.

I love you.

T

8-7-67
Monday, p.m.

Toni —

This day has been a good day. Someone borrowed two packs of cigarettes from my desk at work; who, I don't know. I guess I don't really care, but everybody else is treating it as a matter of life or death. They go to all ends to convince me of their innocence, and one of them to convince himself. . . .

Be gentle,

T

Tuesday p.m.

Toni —

. . . I would write you about what I did today, but it would be deathly boring — it was for me. . . .

T

Toni —

. . . *Seven Storey Mountain* is Merton's autobiography — a remarkably interesting and well-written book, for a cleric. The
only thing about it that irritates me is an occasional passage of
moralistic denunciation of the evils of worldly life, sermonizing
of the worst kind disguised as confessional self-reproach. That
and an occasional collapse of logic in arguments in which logic
has no place. For instance: the devil says, "The great misery of
the world proves that no merciful God exists." Merton replies,
". . . the fact that God has not destroyed us, or let us destroy
ourselves, completely, proves the infinite mercy of God." This
sounds good, if a bit glib, and the devil sulks off, a beaten cur.
However, look closely at the argument: it does not concern the
existence of God, but rather the disputed mercifulness of God
who is tacitly assumed to exist. Both the devil and the angel
need God in order to prove the rightness of their respective
prejudices; God is the raison d'etre (sp?) for both good and
evil. And by definition, good is good is God and therefore tri-
umphs over evil which is evil which is the devil. But if there is
no God, the question of His infinite mercy becomes a moot point;
i.e., if there is no God who punishes the world mercifully for its
sins, no causal relation between sin and misery (in the theological sense of the words) can be demonstrated. The great misery of the world proves either (1) that God is infinitely merciful or (2) that God does not exist, and corollarily, neither do
sin and misery insofar as we cannot sin against a non-existent
Being nor can a non-existent Being impose misery, however
mercifully, upon us. Whether one answers (1) or (2) on his
application to the Great Beyond seems to me a matter of personal temperament. . . .

T

8-14-67

Darling —

. . . Formal rules are the embalmment of common sense or the sanctification of prejudice — in either case a bad thing, for they rob the one of vitality and give the other an authority it does not deserve. . . .

Love & Peace
Tim

8-18-67

Toni —
. . . I cannot condone Brown's and Carmichael's advocacy of violence, I disagree with SNCC's interpretation of the Arab-Israeli problem, and I abhor the riots in Newark and Detroit only slightly less than I abhor the conditions which gave rise to them. C. disagrees with me about much of this — he justifies the riots as necessary (which in a way they are *ex facto*, but necessity is a poor arbiter for the claims of human justice against dehumanizing violence); C. also feels that Brown's view is the only effective way to reach the people, that King's non-violent resistance is an esoteric doctrine divorced from political and social realities. C. accuses me of being a "reformist" rather than a true radical, but I think he misses this point: that what I believe and propose in a way transcends reform and revolution in seeking to establish a new and encompassing principle, namely nonviolence, which repudiates all previous standards by which social and political change have been judged. "Keep thyself first in peace and then thou wilt be able to bring others to peace." . . .

Tim

25 August, 1967

Art,
. . . I read recently a pamphlet by Thomas Merton entitled "Blessed Are the Meek: The Christian Roots of Nonviolence."

I thought it an excellent exposition of one aspect of pacifism —
that of total personal commitment to the principle of nonviolence — and I recommend it urgently to your attention if you
have not already seen it. . . .

Love and peace
Tim

25 August, 1967

Dear Parents,

. . . I got a letter — a very nice letter — from Judge Porter, who
is back from his vacation. I am working on an answer now.

Toni will not be coming down on the weekend of the 2nd
August, since she is planning to go to Art Kanegis' wedding in
D.C. on that day. I also received an invitation, but due to cir-
cumstances beyond my control, I shall not be going. . . .

Love and peace
Tim

26 August, 1967

Sunshine —

. . . There was an interesting letter to the Editor of the *Times*
on Wednesday, which asserted that our cities aren't worth sav-
ing because they are obsolete. This may fit with McLuhan's
thesis of the retribalization of civilization through electronic
communications, in that the city, as a discrete social and political unit, may lose its essential identity under the impact of
instantaneous communications, because now everybody in the
U.S. knows what is going on in New York as well as any New
Yorker does, and a nation of New Yorkers means the same thing
as having no New Yorkers at all. That is the abstract, theoretical

side of the contention; on the concrete side, witness the migration to the suburbs, etc. . . .

Love and peace
Tim

4th Sept., 1967

Toni —

I got a letter from you today (or yesterday; boundaries in time dissolve in the acid of memory, and the gracious fatal curve of day arches in to meet its end in its and another day's beginning) finally (it had been a week almost I think, the last one saying you were going home and you love me; and I not hearing, not knowing whether you were there indeed or not yet, for some monstrous and unthinkable reason somewhere not there and not here — I wondered and fretted and worried and struggled not to hope or pray or wish for a letter, but to wait patiently, un-anxiously like a speckled hen warming a smooth white stone), and I was thankful for the letter's final and belated coming and for the letter itself, its words — your words — like order and hope and life itself sent again for the redeemed but unrepentant me (and love does not repent of its words and breath and being, though all things accuse, convict, scorn it in its irredeemable and homeless folly). I repent not but cry aloud in the joyous syllabic thunder of love and this letter, lost and impersonal there being nothing more alien and friendless than the base of our being and its cry, and rend the unmoral, eternal and infinite sky which would shed its immortal, ever-mutable and changing clouds and color before the forked flash of truth in three words and syllables: I love you, and refuse to be serious or grim, apology-laden harbinger of false repudiation of a false echo of being though the bird-red and burning stigma of folly and uncouth honesty be scored to my love, seeking to bind and blind, and shackle and manacle the best and most aspiring, never-failing hope and love within and among and between me and you and all men. *I love you* shakes the earth, and man quakes in his secret and submerged being beneath the kind and terrible assault

34

and impact of this my and man's only true and generous gift to you and to himself in others (and others in himself just as you in me are not a separate part but completely swallowed and consumed and transformed by and in my nature, it by and in you, though always and however much you remain completely and indubitably you, and I me, apart, other, distinct and particular, rejoicing in and exalting my own and your and each man's unimpingeable uniqueness and island-isolated identity). . . .

I am reading *A Fable*, a mindless wandering of a mind by Faulkner, through the phantasmagoric miasma of war and peace and religion and hope in its eternal and futile defiance against the world — a monstrous book, a book of wisdom hid so deep and unrecoverable that it reaches past our intellectualization and imagination and seizes something deeper and unrecoverable except by the unrecoverable wisdom of this book — spirits speaking to and grappling with spirits whom we steadfastly deny except that our souls are torn with and by the conflict, and we say there are no such things as earthquakes our homes and lands and safety slide with a deep roar to new and unlearned but felt wisdom and stability. . . .

Peace,
T

1 October, 1967

Toni —

. . . My right little toe hurts when I move it, and I'm afraid to take off my shoe to look at it. Later maybe. Of course, I think it's all your fault for not being here to take care of me — or maybe it's my fault for being here where you can't take care of me — or maybe it's nobody's fault, and that's the worst possibility of all, our being separated and no one to take the blame because they're all concerned about bigger and badder evils. And a little goodness when it isn't there, and should be, isn't important enough to concern them. . . .

T

3 October, 1967

Parents —

Judy should read Agee's *A Death in the Family* for growing-up. . . . Should I plan to go into medicine? Med. School would be quite a strain and I'm not sure about the A.M.A. Also, I'd have a lot of chemistry and biology to catch up with. Just an idea — I think the mind appeals to me more than the body, and history more than histology.

Tim

4 October, 1967

Arthur —

. . . I am very much troubled by some observations . . . about the Peace Movement. It seems to me that too many of the people in it are in it only in form and not in spirit. The spirit I am thinking of is for me pacifism, but it doesn't have to be that for everyone; more generally, I mean a spirit of commitment, both to the objectives of the movement, on one hand, and to a personal pattern of life which conforms to these wider objectives. No tyrant was ever a democrat, no matter how much he spoke of freedom, and no slave truly understands freedom unless he knows and understands its price and responsibilities, however much he may long for it. The Peace Movement is threatened with a disunity, not of goals — for these remain clear if the method for their attainment still eludes us — but, more seriously, of method or spirit. And I do not mean a lack of unity among the different methods proposed and the different spirits prevailing within the movement, but a more basic disunity or disparity between spirit and commitment within the individuals who comprise the movement. We are threatened, in other words, with becoming, consciously or unconsciously, dishonestly or honestly, an assembly of hypocrites. We say, many of us, that such and such a condition is evil, that such and such a goal is good; this is the spirit which binds us, not in commitment, but in the possibility of commitment. For it is what comes after the good and the evil have been defined and agreed upon that determines the grain of activism. Do we practice what we preach? Or, do we, advocating peace, resort to violence in our advocacy? and advocating freedom, refuse to face the real threat to our security which freedom brings? and advocating love, hate the haters more than they hate us? . . . If we preach love and freedom and peace, we must first love, be free, be peaceful — or better yet not preach at all but let love and peace and freedom speak for themselves in our actions. It is a slow journey, and a painful, discouraging one; do we have the strength for it? . . .

> Love, Peace, and all good
> and gentle things,
> Tim

6 October, 1967

Parents,

. . . Toni writes every day as I do to her. She seems a little discouraged with herself in her schoolwork, but this probably doesn't mean too much as most college students seem to have the same feeling. Toni sent me a copy of the Earlham *Post* . . . and it was at any rate nostalgically pleasant to read about all the old Earlhamites, most of whose names are unfamiliar to, or unremembered by, me. . . .

> Love and peace,
> Tim

6 October

Toni Darling,

This is your friendly institution hospital. Please be quiet — the patients need their rest. See the patients resting comfortably; please be quiet so you don't disturb them. See the doctors. They

37

are healing the patients; please be quiet, because the doctors must concentrate on their healing; if they are disturbed, they might mix the wrong medicine for the comfortably resting patients. Please be quiet. See the doctors' assistants; they help the doctors heal the patients; please be quiet, for the doctors' assistants are very much concerned for the patients' rest and comfort. Please be quiet. See the cheerful inmate attendants; they care for the patients and see to their every need, especially that they have peace and quiet; so please be quiet. See the hard-working demolition crew; they are tearing down a wall between two wards in the hospital; they are not always here, but they have been for the past week; see them using their sledge hammers, and jackhammers, and chisels, and shovels; hear the brick and plaster and wooden beams falling: fun, fun, fun; the hard-working demolition crew obviously doesn't give a damn about the peace and quiet of the hospital.

That's how it's been for the last three days: bang, bang, clatter, crash; screech, thud, boom; ratatata, sigh, screech, hissss, crash. The shaking of the foundations. Sure enough. And dust! . . .

I love you.

T

7 October, 1967

Dear Family,

. . . You might send some money (please?) as soon as you can because through a misunderstanding on my part I find that I have none and it's going to be a little tight cigarette-wise this week. Of course, I would like to hear how things are too. . . .

Love and peace,
Tim

Toni —

. . . The most difficult encounters, it seems, are with people who pass you in darkness, somehow asking, needing your help or understanding or humanness and presence. You come upon each other suddenly, there is a moment of meeting. Fleeting, insubstantial, it comes and is gone before it has a chance to become separate from the stream of life, but not before that moment has interrupted the flow and upset the smooth course and meaning of existence. That disturbance lingers as something incomplete, something which will probably never be completed, fulfilled, but only concluded without satisfaction or meaning. Encounters like this leave a hole in the continuity of life; we never meet each other face to face, but in these uneven and incomplete moments we do not even look, or dare to look. We are so bound to the meaning of our own existence, so anchored to what is, not familiar, but meaningful in our lives that a moment of encounter with a stranger who asks or demands or pleads for what we would unhesitatingly give to a friend shakes us from our anchorage or foundation and we find ourselves threatened with uncontrol, unmeaning, uncertainty, floating on the sea of existence. This is our fault though it is not our fault; it is our weakness as human beings and as beings. For being imperfect as beings, being incomplete and unselfsufficient products, not causes, of our being, we must constantly cling to other beings, other separate realities, as though by giving part of our being to others and part of our incomplete existence to others, we could make our own being less insecure, less conditional and incomplete. For us meaning is what we know, the familiar, the friendly. To attempt to project a part of our being into the unfamiliar and unknown is to risk a disintegration of our identity; it is also to risk a greater growth of our identity and meaning, but only under the right conditions. The unknown and unknowing OTHER must also seek to know, not merely to touch and leave, unknown and unknowing. The OTHER must be willing to become less other, more a part of our self. I don't know whether I've said anything that means anything to you — it means much to me and troubles me, and I could explain it if I could talk to you and you could question me and smile when you understand. I love you.

T.

19 October, 1967

Mother,

. . . Study conditions are miserable — I get a severe headache just thinking about studying in the dorm at night. I need quiet and I need more time — as it is I have to stop usually about nine o'clock. Hopefully I'll be up in the honor cell house within the next couple of months — private room, desk, late hours — it will be paradise compared to the barn.

I really think that the humanities are more my style than medicine. . . . History is still to my mind the noblest of the academic vocations, combining within its range all other fields of human endeavor. There is nothing which is not history, and until the computers take over completely, history will be one of the humanities and not a science.

Have you ever thought how wonderful it would be to be transported back in time to another age, a previous civilization, and with your advanced knowledge of science and history to change the course of history? — I have. But I think at the same time that I would not want to receive a visitor from a future time so much as I would like to have an ancient Egyptian pharaoh or a Greek philosopher or a medieval schoolman revived to life somehow so that he could tell me how and why he lived. And perhaps I could do the same service to a future generation of historians by coming back to life a thousand years from now to set the twentieth century before their eyes. I am not interested in the future very much; but I am interested in the future's interest in us. . . .

Timothy

20 October
Friday a.m.

Ellie —

You may be planning to go to the march in Washington. . . . So I'll tell you what I think about it, and you will be able to judge, either from your own observation or from what others tell you, whether I am right or wrong.

40

First — violence. There may be violence at the march. Violence can almost always be avoided, but only if people are intent on avoiding it. With thousands of people gathered in a small area, nonviolence ceases to be a personal commitment; it becomes a social act and a social duty. If violence breaks out, it is not nonviolence which has failed, but it is we who have failed nonviolence. Bend a stick and it will approach a breaking point; bend it too far and it will break; you cannot hope to bend a stick without risking breaking it. In every act of nonviolent resistance, in every act of nonviolent civil-disobedience, there is the risk of breaking the stick, the risk of violence. A peaceful intention is not enough — you must know what you are about, what you are up against. In Washington you will be up against the police — they are human beings who, because of their professional experience, have an early breaking point. You are not protesting the police, you are not demonstrating against the police, but the most immediate and palpable obstacle which you will face will be the police. If the nonviolent demonstration against the most brutal form of violence conceivable — war — turns into a violent demonstration against the police, you are lost. You have failed nonviolence. You have failed to protest the war, and you have failed to live nonviolently. If there is violence at the march, I shall hear no excuses. The demonstrators will have failed either in intent or in knowledge — they will have either accepted the necessity or unavoidability of violence or failed to know when the stick will break. In the first case, I will not conscience (condone) them; I cannot support an attitude against war, or against a particular war, which takes the principle of war as its own. At best, I don't agree with them; at worst, I think they are hypocrites.

Second — the image. One of the Ashland radio announcers is convinced that the march on Washington is part of a communist conspiracy; one of the inmates here said that it was going to be a "hippie demonstration." I know that it is not the former. If it is the latter, it will fail. What is the movement? It is not part of an international conspiracy; it is not a hippie happening; it is not a political party; it is not an arm of Black Power; it is not a fad. But what *is* it? It is, on the one hand, one of the poles in the only true political dialogue in America today — the dialogue between the Establishment and the New Left. Republican Party and Democratic Party have little meaning politically. The difference in potential between them is almost nil; the November elections are very nearly meaningless. On the other hand, the movement has no corporate identity. It has many faces — Black Power, hippie, anti-conscription, pacifist, revolutionary, nonconformist, anarchist, civil rights, even communist. But none of these faces so predominates that it can be called *the* face of the movement. Are there any characteristics of all these faces which are common to a majority of the movement? Is nonviolence an essential tenet of the movement as a whole? Look at Rap Brown. Is violent revolution a basic goal of the movement as a whole? Look at B. Spock, look at me. Is freedom a basic tenet of the movement as a whole? Perhaps. But freedom is not, cannot be an end in itself. It is what is done with freedom that is essential, and no two groups in the movement agree about the uses of freedom. What is essential to the movement as a whole? Opposition — opposition to the war, to all wars; to conscription, to military conscription, to radical injustice, and to social prejudice; to suppression of civil liberty, to suppression of freedom. The movement is one of opposition, and the alternatives offered by the movement are many and contradictory: Burn, Baby, Burn — Let the people decide — Black Power — Flower Power — Turn On — Peace — Revolution — Nonviolence.

Third — nonviolence. I believe that the principle of nonviolence must lie at the root of New Left opposition to the Establishment, not because there is a god-given precept for pacifism but because a belief in violence is the source and pervading tone of Establishment power. Rap Brown's appeal to fight injustice with violence is a cry of frustration — it is no real alternative to injustice but a blind reaction to spiritual torture. The only real alternative to injustice is justice, and justice cannot be reconciled with violence. Some form of violence lies at the root of all human injustices. Where the assertion of justice fails — as it has and will often fail — there are two courses: one is the course of violence and frustration, the course of Rap Brown; the other is the course of human compassion and a justice deeper than law, the course of Martin Luther King. The cry of violence against violence, the cry of injustice against injustice will fail and fail miserably. It has failed throughout the history of mankind. The cry of compassion, of human love, is a weaker one: Man is not used to calling on what is most human in him to fight his battles; it has always been the animal in him who has held the day. In this age the animal in man may destroy man himself, and yet we sound the call for violence. Nonviolence only, if anything, stands a chance of reversing the escalation of hatred in the war of prejudice. It will be hard, it may not succeed, but only the greatest revolution in history can now make a significant difference; only the overthrow of violence will restore humanness in man and justice in men's lives. If there is not this potential for nonviolent commitment to the future in the movement, I want nothing of it. But nonviolence is there; it is a small voice and is nearly drowned by the easy and superficially revolutionary cries of "get you a gun." There is nothing revolutionary about violence — violence is as old as man. If there is to be a revolution, let it be a real one — a revolution against violence.

Love and peace,
Timothy

10.30.67

Parents —

Forgive the long silence. Things are going particularly well. I give you three guesses as to where I am just now — no, not in the hospital; no, not in the dining room; that's right, I'm now in the honor cell house. It is a pleasant (what an understatement!) place compared to the dorm. . . .

Love and peace,
Tim

11.8.67

Darling,

For today's discussion, we are presented with two problems suggested by Aristotle. First, the problem of love and the motives for love. Second, the alleged inferiority of women to men.

I submit, with all due respect, that Aristotle knew not of what he spoke. If the motive of love is utility alone, then that is not

43

love. If the motive of love is pleasure alone, that is not love. If the motive of love is virtue alone, then that also is not love. In other words then, if a pretense of love is used as a guise for other motives and desires, that is not love but a counterfeit of love. Aristotle defines utility, pleasure, and virtue as more or less absolute metaphysical quantities: he then identifies them as possible components of love or friendship. But he does not so define "love" itself. What Aristotle defines as love derived from virtue (goodness, excellence) is tantamount to love as nothing but a derivative of virtue. He does not consider love as an absolute metaphysical quantity — and in this omission he is quite right; where he errs is in defining utility, pleasure, and virtue as such quantities. Aristotle would certainly object to a definition of a virtue based on utility or on pleasure — such a virtue is not real virtue. But he does not scruple to put love on the level of a dependent and derivative quality. What he means is that (what he could only mean and make sense is that) a love or friendship based on utility or pleasure alone is not a virtuous love; a love based on virtue is (by definition) virtuous. But in Aristotle's sense, I submit that love — pure love — exists on the same metaphysical level as utility, pleasure, or virtue — that is, they exist in the uncertain realm of metaphysical forms but never appear in life as pure quantities. Love is as much a real thing (and independent) in life as is virtue — it exists in man in combination with other qualities, including utility, pleasure, and virtue. No love or friendship is based on utility, pleasure, or virtue — it is based on itself but exists with the others. I love you. Take that as an objective statement. Certainly I derive great pleasure from loving you; but if mere pleasure were my motive, I could undoubtedly do better by creating a playboy image. (I here take "pleasure" in a narrow sense of sensual and social satisfaction; in a broader sense, taking "pleasure" to mean the total complex of needs, desires, and standards which constitute my psyche and their relationship to what pleases me — in the extreme, this is taken to mean that anything I do pleases me because I would not do anything that is displeasing to me — I could only have pleasure in loving you as I do.) Likewise, I suppose that I derive some utilitarian satisfaction from loving you — I concede this only to pacify Aristotle, for in all that is good for me in our relationship, there is the same good for you. We do not use each other as objects but as people. It is a reciprocating "use" which becomes deeper than object-use because of its reciprocating nature. Furthermore, in my love for you there is virtue — a belief in the goodness, the everlastingness of us and of each other. But none of these things is the determinant of my love for you. That love is itself, and though it partakes of the other human motives, its basic nature — as love *per se* — is not impugned. As I have said, this is shaky ground — "true love" is real no more and no less than "true virtue." If we accept one, we are constrained to accept the other. If we accept nothing — we still accept the absoluteness of nothingness — we are then no better or worse off than before. . . .

I am too tired to give extensive consideration to the second question. . . .

Tonistim

11.13.67

Toni —

. . . General Hershey, czar of the S.S.S., has been raising hell about us. I'm not sure how I feel about on-campus military recruitment. It conflicts with my conception of the purpose of education, but, on the other hand, I may be prejudiced. If a major role of a college education is to train people for jobs, then every kind of recruitment is justifiable. At any rate, a majority consensus on the problem should determine the institution's policy to a certain extent. This should not prohibit demonstrations of protest against certain kinds of recruitment, but, in all honesty, physical prevention of recruitment is not justified where a majority have invited or allowed recruiters to recruit. Has the question arisen at Earlham? I wish I were there with you.

Tonistim

Darling —

. . . Last night I went to a high school football game with the Librarian who is a dear kind soul. The Ashland high school team is very good this year — they're playing in the state finals next weekend. The game was a complete routing — Ashland won 42-0. But it was good to get out for a while. It was cold.

It was a very odd feeling sitting in the stands surrounded by high school age people. What a loud, insecure lot they are. The boys, awkward on their first dates, trying so hard to impress, failing utterly to communicate. Manfully smoking forbidden cigarettes, speaking more to other boys than to the girls they were escorting. One boy was obviously the first among his uncertain peers. He was with no girl, but strutted and gesticulated pretentiously for the entire crowd. He wore a short-sleeve shirt despite the weather and talked in a loud boastful voice to anyone who would listen. Self-conscious and uncertain, he proclaimed the nascent importance of his manhood to a world too involved in their own growing up to take notice.

The girls, some of them beautiful in the first bloom of their sex, some heavily made-up, mouths too sharp, eyes too vivid, their young bodies too perfect imitations of Hollywood goddesses, some still awkward and ungainly, grinning foolishly at foolish boys who paid more attention to their generic womanhood than to their individual personalities. One girl was exquisite, finely chiseled features with just a thin, elusive veil of cosmetics, tall and thin, carrying her body with a poise that showed less arrogance than natural self-respect. She was alone, but from her aloofness and the distant look of bitter joy on her face, I guessed that she was proud of one of the football players. Another girl sat between two less beautiful friends. Her small lips (her mouth still had the awkward, disjointed looseness of a child) were a fluorescent purple, her eyes green. She wore a fashionable little hat over her fashionable boyish haircut. (I ought to say coiffure for poetic consistency, but I don't know how to spell it.)

So many, all the familiar and remembered kinds of half-men and not-quite-women. One girl reminded me of Amy — a tall, loosed-jointed body and a wide, imperfectly beautiful and intriguing face. A fat boy, lonely, viewed the crowd with disdain and sadness. Uncertain, awkward, boastful, foolish, happy-sad, confused and arrogant, self-conscious, important, inadequate. Ah,

46

days of youth, years of growing! Every new and innocent joy lay before us. One older boy — no, a man, — obviously past high school (past joy and wonder) walked with a girl through the crowd — she, too blondly unbeautiful, destined to be an unhappy wife to a brutal husband.

The girls were on the whole more aware than the boys — more aware of their destiny and fate, their beauty and their bashfulness. Dreams of future colored by the half-sad joys and wonders of present. Oh, foolish youth, oh, grand masquerade of beauty! Dream of tomorrow, live for today. The girls were fresh in the bloom of womanhood, but only one in a crowd of painted and unpainted, exquisite and over-done, beautiful and unbeautiful, would not turn out to be insipid, uninteresting, and deathly banal bourgeois — that is their lot. The poet takes delight in the form and appearance of beauty, but one conversation with a youthful Helen destroys the myth. Empty, empty. The philosopher finds no joy.

I love you.

T.

11.19.67

Toni —

. . . I had decided that I was going to take the step of repudiating the conscription system and the military establishment, and I was fairly certain that I would go to jail for it, long before I met you. The summer before you came to Earlham was decisive in my intellectual ordeal, and when I came back to school that fall I refused to submit the academic information required for a student deferment. My meeting and falling in love with you was a difficult experience, but I think it was somehow destined that I would involve another person whom I loved and knew as I love and know myself in my act of defiance and assertion. My loving you was also an act of defiance — I defied common sense, simple decency, and conventional responsibility in order to commit myself to you at that point in my life. I knew that soon, before we could really learn to know each other, we would be

47

separated for a long time. I knew that I was going to hurt you, and, though I despised myself for that necessity, I felt that somehow the pain of being hurt and the pain of guilt would not destroy what we had invested in each other. At first I had thought to leave you gently, to avoid pulling you into my vale of tears, but I know now that would have been a coward's answer. We had surprised me by the mystifying ease with which we came to understand and accept and finally love each other. I was disturbed because the sudden perfection of our relationship hit me as a revelation and destroyed all hope of an easy way out. I knew that I had to hurt you because I loved you — that the pain of separation would be nothing compared to what we might have lost had we made an easy parting. No matter what happens, when I leave here there will be something between us to build on; it may be a lonely painful thing because of its long exile, but it will be there and we will make it wonderful. If — I say if — we can make it through these years, we will make it forever. If we fail, it will be my failing because I miscalculated or wasn't strong enough. I love you with all my being, like it or not, and this being includes the pain and suffering. I am crucifying you as I am crucified, and the crucifixion is an act of love and awful responsibility. . . .

T.

11.22.67

Toni darling, i love you.

. . . Yesterday I was talking with a man, and through his words I saw into his intellectual soul. It didn't strike me then, nor for a while afterwards, but at night as I lay thinking of it I comprehended clearly what I had seen. I was terrified. Imagine if you can a soul which has been stripped of every shred of idealism; it is a black pit; it is an evil thing. Long years of living have worn away all hope. Only resignation is left. Deceit, compromise, an unlovely fear of change. It is the worst manifestation of a practical mind, so practical that every truth is defined by expediency, and compromise is not even a meeting between ideals and practical considerations — it is rather a balancing of practical questions — expediency, utility, fear.

T.

11.25.67

Toni —

. . . I get very miserably upset when people are angry. Lately I have come up against some people who have nothing but contempt for pacifism. Their frustration is a binding, choking cloud of confusion in conversation. They have no capacity for comprehending an idea which conflicts with their own ideas. The brotherhood of man means nothing — less than nothing. If nationalism necessarily involves the abrogation of human bonds, then perhaps the anarchists are right. If a man is American, Russian, Chinese, or Nigerian before he is human, then I reject all national designation. I am an unwilling member of a political society in a system of political societies which subjugates my human identity to my national designation. If the accident of my birth is to supersede the fact of my human existence, then my birth is a crime. Man means nothing anymore. Man does not exist. It is a trick of capricious fate that the citizens of all nations happen to be men. This merely confounds our situation. It means that we cannot kill off all non-Americans without compunction because some deluded souls insist that a man is a man no matter what his nationality. This may or may not be true — obviously it is a fact of no importance. The fact that a man is an American (Russian, Chinaman, Nigerian) means that he has a greater right to life, truth, and power than any non-American (non-Russian, non-Chinese . . .). Bah! Hitler had the same idea; his mistake was to recognize the inevitable consequence of his philosophy and to act on it.

T.

Dear Parents,

I am sorry I haven't written. I am weary in mind and soul, and the weariness conquers also an unwilling and refractory flesh. I am unable, unwilling, to do anything but read and write a letter each evening to Toni. Even that letter is a task sometimes.

My isolation is complete — social, emotional, existential. Existential isolation is reflected in an attitude that nothing that one thinks, feels, or does is related to anything else. My sorrow, my joy are pebbles cast in a dark well; no light rides the ripples of my feelings.

Today is Richard's birthday. There is no way I can excuse, deny, or obliterate my not writing to him earlier in the week. I thought of him, of all of you, and when I noticed that the tenor of my thought was not predominantly longing or fondness or happiness, but guilt at not writing, not being able to force myself to the simple, self-justifying discipline of writing, I thought I had learned something new and important — something about myself. Something to change. So happy birthday to Richard — may the day have taught him as much as I have learned. . . .

Love and peace,
Tim

7 December, 1967

Toni —

. . . I'm one big emotional knot inside. It ties up all my energies, all my visions. I can do nothing. I'm helpless in the face of my own confusion. I've been this way for the past two weeks. I have to talk to you before the knot will become untangled. I can't say it in letters — they're too slow, too unrevealing. I have to see you when you hear my questions, my doubts, my confusion, my affirmation. It is too much for me to cope with alone, but that is no weakness — the universe of my love and doubt and life and faith has you at the center. I want to — I have to — understand this universe; to do that I have to understand you. I love this universe of my being because I love you. You have asked me to tell you about everything — the pain, the joy, the frustration, the anger. It is all there; I haven't told you the smallest part of it. All of it is bound up with you. You know it if you know yourself — and me. Will I ever be able to tell you? I think so, if. . . . The question is when. While I am here, bound within the iron and concrete correlatives of my shame, doubt, guilt, life, love, affirmation? We have to try. It is a matter of life and death — my life in here, your life out there during these two years. Will we have to wait until I am free? Will I ever be free? January is a long way off. Even then, will we have enough time even to begin? All life is beginning; all existence is becoming. We have to talk, Toni. We can't postpone it. The undiscovered, the unexamined, the denied and refused of our relationship has built up too long behind the wall of our silence. That is not our fault — conditions have not been ideal. I would give anything to have made a different decision so that things could have been easier for us. But if I had decided differently, I would have given up everything, become nothing. I had to choose between living in the fire of my identity and dying on the comfortable altar of propriety. I chose to live, to love; I risked both life and· love knowing that without the risk there would be nothing worth living for, nothing that deserved to love or be loved. Do you understand? I did it for myself because myself is all that I have to offer to you, to the world. . . .

I love you.
Peace,
T.

12.12.67

Family —

. . . I've received approximately thirty Christmas cards from unknown friends and sympathizers from (literally) around the world.

Two nonreligious objectors here have agreed to be drafted. Neither is of the same political-conscientious persuasion which characterizes members of the Movement. I am sorry to say that I fear both of them will be sent directly to Vietnam, to kill and be killed. It is regrettable but unavoidable that one's insistence on the individual's right to live as he chooses is accompanied by a corollary principle that the individual must also be free to die as he chooses. Is this choice? The concept of free will is only superficially appreciated by most people. Whether one believes the universe of life to be the creation of an intelligent will or a chaotic, unpredictable "happening" on a cosmic level, free will loses out in either case — in the first, because the wrong choice means alienation from reality; in the second, because any choice is meaningless.

I here paraphrase a statement I read somewhere (leader of the Left opposition in France, I believe) : Anyone who is not a revolutionary in his youth gives the impression of being senile. As always, the United States lags behind Europe in important political and social tendencies. The revolutionary tradition of Europe in the 1920's and '30's is only now being adopted and adapted by American youth. More power.

Love and Peace,
Tim

12.16.67

Family —

. . . I . . . got a nice letter from Judge Porter. . . . It is very encouraging that we are able to speak so fully and so frankly with each other. He is a wonderful person.

Love and peace,
T.

Dear Family —

Just a short letter to tell you that I am still here — which will come as no surprise to you, I'm sure. . . .

Love and peace,
Tim

12.19.67

Mother —

. . . Today I started learning the routine in the laboratory of the hospital. The present lab technician will be leaving soon hopefully (you can bet that he's hoping!). When he does leave, I will take his place. I hope that I will be able to continue assisting in surgery as it is more interesting than pouring blood and urine from one bottle to another all day. But the lab work will fill the day and the experience may prove valuable. . . .

Love and peace,
Tim

Thursday 1.4.68

Darling —

Things have happened without me — like in a novel. Only they have happened through people I love, through you. I have to talk with somebody — but it's like trying to talk with a character from a novel. Everything moves independently of me, without me. I feel helpless and foolish. The characters speak their lines and make their gestures. I sit and watch, powerless to move, to interfere, to influence, hoping only to understand. Intellectually I have understood; my mind has accepted, analyzed, and catalogued the cold, gray facts. But the rest of me is still bewildered. It is as though someone came up to me and said, "A woman has died in an accident." For a moment I am at a loss. Then I say, "I'm sorry. Is there anything I can do?" "Yes," she says, "come to her. She was your mother."

The first revelation falls into place. A process of the mind summons knowledge, reason, sympathy into analytical play. I can understand the death of a woman. It happens all the time. My concern, my sympathy are of the intellect. The second revelation summons all the hidden reserves of being — emotion, love, memory, pain. I am lost. My mother is dead. That can happen only once. It can never be understood. Never be explained. I have to talk with you. The need to talk, feel, hear you is like a slowly mounting tide. Imperceptibly it rises and engulfs. I feel like screaming at times. I need you. A part of my life is suddenly and arbitrarily denied me. I am lost, and like a marooned survivor, half dead and delirious. I hear the distant noise and movement of my life — my life — going on without me. The better half of me is in and with you. It is beyond my control; its actions and feelings are even sometimes beyond my knowledge.

. . . If your letters spoke with your voice, if they had the texture of your skin and the warmth of your body, if they could move with your gestures and smile with your lips, if I could see in them your face, touch your hair, if I could be sure that they were saying all the things that can't be said with words, if . . . — then I would be happy. But there is only one Toni. And the letters are a poor counterfeit. I love you. The mind is a frail vessel. Breathe on it and it cracks. Touch it and it shatters. I love you.

T.

Friday 1.5.68

Darling —

I remember reading some months ago of a similar, though in a way more dismaying, incident. A woman had plunged off a road into a river near a bridge. She managed to get out of the car and climb onto its roof. She stood there as the car slowly

54

sank, calling for help and crying that she couldn't swim. A number of cars stopped along the road and there was a small crowd of pedestrians on the bridge. They watched. Only a ten-year-old boy, who couldn't swim, tried to do anything. He ran about trying to persuade an adult to jump into the water to try to save the woman. It wouldn't have been very difficult — the car was not far from the bank and the current was not swift. Nobody moved. They watched. The car went under and the woman drowned. The spectators.

The reason this incident is more dismaying than the other is that the woman's death was absolutely gratuitous. She did not have to die. No one had to die. To stand by and watch another die is not an offense merely against conscience or decency; it is an act against the very nature of humanity. The spectator mentality — . What would I have done? To suppose that my pacifism, my belief in nonviolence, automatically proscribes me from putting my arms forcefully about another person to prevent him from injuring or killing another person would be patently absurd. To a certain extent, the distinction between violence and legitimate force is one of motive and mind. For me, this "certain extent" does not extend to ignoring another person; but it does include physically restraining him if I think such action, such force, is called for. I think this is rather apparent. My conscientious preference in all cases is to talk. Words can do good things, but you have to give them a chance. I do recognize, however, that in many instances, verbal communication is limited in its effectiveness. Beyond this there is physical force. There are, I think, three levels of physical demonstration — violence, restraint, and love or friendship. The first — violence — arises out of an inability or unwillingness to consider persons as persons; that is, as human beings like oneself. Thus, just as one does not talk to a table or fence, so one cannot talk with someone whom one considers to be little more than a table or fence — an object. . . .

The second level of physical demonstration — restraint — is a hybrid. It combines the purely human aspect of concern for a person as a person with the temporary need to treat the person as an object. Thus one holds onto a person who is about to jump off a bridge, just as one would grasp and steady a tottering vase. One catches a child who is about to fall down the stairs; one restrains a man who is about to injure someone. The distinction between force (restraint) and violence is essentially this: violence arises out of a distorted view of man's subjective nature; frustration and anger erupt in physical gestures or actions which have no meaning for — which do not communicate to — the person being acted upon. Restraint, as a variety of force, is secondary to communication; it never forms the basis of a relationship. The relationship between a soldier and his enemy is based on mutual violence. Their hostility, their desire to kill each other, is the basis of their relationship — they treat each other as objects (as living obstacles), living, but objects nonetheless. One cannot treat a person with violence — the person ceases to be a human being: where is all his wonder and past and complexity and promise, his love and his blindness, when one can knock him over as one pushes down a snowman? Restraint is ambiguous. In the eternal conflict between mind and body, we rarely find one or the other alone. They exist inextricably together. An act — any act — reflects this union. Where the body dominates, where the object holds sway, there is no meaning except the meaning which the mind sees in an object. Only the mind, only an act dominated by the mind, can have meaning in itself. Spectator and participator — body and mind. Rape is violence; prostitution is an ambiguous form of restraint; marriage, with love, with or without the ceremony, is love. . . .

T.

Monday 1. 15. 68

Toni —

About the Peace Committee. I think we cannot expect it to be anything more than a free forum for discussion, especially at Earlham which is more academically oriented than many colleges. If it does not fulfill even this function, then it is failing miserably. Last year it barely managed. The exodus, which started before last year, is a principal cause of this disintegration. The group we had during my first year was remarkable — it will never be duplicated. . . . We were a strong nucleus. Gradually it has fallen apart. Earlham — Richmond — has little to offer. B. is in San Francisco; M. is with *Ramparts;* R. is at M.S.U.; E. is in Florida; J. M. is in Philly; J. H. is everywhere — bigger and better things.

Maybe in a couple of years there will be another nucleus. Where patterns have not been institutionalized, where tradition is weak and in the process of building, where roles have not become established, it is personalities which determine the direction of a group. Art was the guiding spirit — but it was us of the nucleus whom he guided. We are gone now, scattered to the winds, and Art has withdrawn into his responsibilities for Suzy. . . .

I never felt particularly alienated at Earlham. I felt more alienated from some of the students than from the faculty and administration. But I think alienation is a real and complex problem for many college students. The single most telling criticism of college education is, I think, the inability of curriculum to meet the challenge of life-at-present. College is no longer viewed as a training for the future — it is part of the future, part of life. What I learn now must not only relate to what I will become but to what I am.   I love you.   T.

Sunday 1.21.68

Darling —

. . . You shouldn't expect too much help from me on your perfect government kick. I got disgusted with that long ago. Any government that would work like the textbook description says it works would be a vast improvement over anything we have now. But it won't happen. But go ahead. Maybe you'll come up with something. . . .

Love and peace,
T.

Monday 1.22.68

Dear parents —

. . . The pressures — many of them self-imposed — are beginning to be unbearable. I feel a kind of crisis approaching. An essential, though only marginally important, aspect of my crisis of self is an emotional and physical explosion of some kind. In this context, I'm not sure how to handle it. I feel extremely uncomfortable, torn between demands and unsatisfied desires for meaningful events. Everything that happens here affects me on a very superficial level. I need something to touch me deeper, to shake me and involve me.

. . . I'm working on my parole application. I'll turn it in tomorrow.

Love and peace,
Tim

Tuesday 1.23.68

Toni —

Do you think I have a tendency not to look at reality as it is? That might be a problem. But so far, all the "realists" I have known have been nothing more than slaves to a reality which is outside them. In order to face reality, do we have to submit to it? A vision within the self has more power than any man's reality — for it can create and transform the real world. . . .

I am, truly, a stranger in a strange country in this place. I long for all that I have lost, and I am blind to all I have gained. People resist change in their own patterns of concern — I as surely as anybody. How do you talk with someone about motorcycles when your mind is seething with the tragedy of the slums? I guess the answer is to find a subject of common concern. Which means that the bulk of my mind has gone without the challenge of conversation for more than eight months. This place is so mildly, subtly anti-human that sheer frustration is actually a positive reaction to it. A man who does not know where he is cannot be accused of travelling too slowly. Can the sheep be called discourteous who declines to discuss with the lion the sauce with which he is to be eaten? I feel so totally helpless and out of touch here that I have to pinch myself every once in a while to make sure I'm still here.

T.

Darling —

. . . I miss my father. I miss his moodiness and his strength, his refusal to find security in platitudes, in conventional attitudes. My father is a very courageous man. The conflict between his need to work in the framework of the establishment and his integrity, his defiance of the hypocrisy of the establishment, make a great strain on him. His responsibility to us, his family, is a burden which compounds his dilemma. A man who chooses to make a family sacrifices some of his freedom — just how much my father is only now coming to realize. The things he would like to do! The great work he might be doing! If he could be free of the establishment I think he *could* do it — with the support and the respect of the family. But what a dangerous choice!! Is one justified in sacrificing security for meaning when it is the security of six, and not one, people involved? How would Judy and Richard get through college if my father suddenly took an unrespectable job as a minister in the ghetto? A low-paying, unprestigious, insecure job. That, I think, is his real vocation, and my family is existentially responsible for keeping him from it. And my mother? She is a very selfless person. She lives, I think, for my father. But she too has a responsibility to the family. This keeps her from making the dangerous, the damaging, the right decision — to allow my father his freedom. Freedom, in this context, is not an absolute; it is merely one of the terms of the problem. Responsibility is just as important. Frankl says that man's ultimate freedom, which cannot be taken from him by any power on earth, is the freedom to choose one's attitude in a given set of circumstances. The attitude which my father sometimes chooses is, I think, a sign of weakness because it disregards the feelings of those who love him. But it is also a sign of strength because it shows that he has not become blinded to the possibilities of life, possibilities which threaten what he is and which therefore point the way to what he can become. If my father were happy in his job, his situation, I could not respect him as I do. I wish he were able to talk more honestly with my mother, with me. But the guilt, the responsibility are not his alone — I share with him the enormity of his frustrated and unrealized dreams, for what he has given to me might otherwise have gone into the fulfillment of those dreams. . . .   T.

Darling —

What have been the reactions at school concerning the North Korean incident? The atmosphere among the inmates here is preponderantly and, as I see it, recklessly pro-war. I don't think you'd believe some of the things people have said. I certainly find it hard to understand the depth and extent of blind patriotic arrogance which some of my friends here exhibit. . . . Their attitude toward the possibility of total war is ambiguous and, in some cases, clearly ambivalent. One boy said that he "hoped war would break out so that he would be released for military service." Another, who had previously expressed supreme indifference as to whether he might be drafted or not, said that the U.S. should have exterminated North Korea within twenty-four hours after the incident. Another voiced a rather prevalent opinion when he claimed that if Kennedy (JFK) were president, the U.S. would already have taught the Koreans the lesson they deserve; Johnson, on the other hand, is being wishy-washy and indecisive. When I asked one of them whether he was upset by the prospect of a nuclear war, he said that he didn't want a war any more than I did, but "we can't let them get away with a thing like that." It seems to me that these boys have not seriously considered the problem of the consequences of a violent response to the incident. A similar disdain of consequences and a refusal to accept responsibility for anyone except himself are marked characteristics of the inmate's attitude toward life. "Look out for number one" is the prevailing credo. When and if such a doctrine were applied to international affairs, the result would not be good, I think. The attitude of many inmates is a disconcerting parody of "My country, right or wrong." I asked one of them whether the question of the ship's real purpose and location — whether it was in Korean territorial waters — made any difference. He replied, "Absolutely not." This sense of loyalty also marks the pattern of personal relationships among prison inmates. One is committed to defend his buddy whether his buddy is in the right or not. It makes no difference.

Actually, I feel much the same way. I don't care *where* the ship was; I'd simply be happier if no one pushed any buttons. I don't think we'll ever learn whether the ship was in international waters or not. I have no greater faith in the Administration's word of honor than in the blatantly propagandistic Koreans. Six months ago the Korean charge that the C.I.A. was behind it would have struck me as absurd; but then, so would the charge that the C.I.A. was subsidizing the National Student Association. In short, I don't know whom to believe, so I believe no one.

I have a strong feeling of utter detachment from the whole affair — a startling contrast to the near-hysterical fervor with which some of my inmate friends advocate swift and massive retaliation, regardless of the consequences. Vietnam has been the first step. The U.S. has got itself into an uncomfortable position. I feel no particular sympathy for national governments involved. I do hope the crewmen of the ship will be released, preferably through the U.N. or the International Red Cross. As to the ship itself and the "national pride and prestige" of all the nations of the world — I just can't get worked up. . . .

T.

January 28, 1968

Darling —

. . . The question of the morality of society is one of my favorites. For the genesis of my own views, I can't do better than to recommend Reinhold Niebuhr's *Moral Man and Immoral Society*, which I read under Paul Lacey's promptings during my first year at Earlham. I don't know whether I can do an adequate job of explaining Niebuhr's thesis now — it's been so long since I read it and it's a difficult book anyway. I think that your way of going at it — concluding that personal morality can't be applied to nations simply because the actions of nations don't jive with moral actions of persons is legitimate to an extent. However, it doesn't prove that international relations *cannot* be structured along moral lines. To show that, you have to demonstrate certain characteristics of collective-national behavior, as opposed to personal behavior. I'll give a few ideas without trying to answer the question systematically. (1) Jefferson's idea of one morality may have been credible in his day and during the centuries before. It does not satisfy me today because the character of international relations is so radically changed. For one thing, consider the rulers of sixteenth- and seventeenth-century European states. National prestige was embodied in the ruler, and the rulers of all major European states were related by blood to each other. Thus, the action of one nation against another was not only the action of cousin against cousin, but it was also the action of gentleman against gentleman. Of course, there were wars and political disputes then, but these were regarded as the tests of honor between the subjects of noble men — tests, that is to say, of the honor of the rulers by their subjects. Even if that characterization is an oversimplification — which it is — it nonetheless points to an essential difference between the nature of the sixteenth-century nation and the twentieth-century nation.

(2) It seems to me that true morality presupposes individual independence; that is, any form of dependence by one or more persons on another creates a morally abnormal situation. Where this dependence is limited and, as in most interpersonal relationships, emotional or psychological in content, the contradiction is not so great as to preclude moral choices; i.e., choices based on concern for what is good or bad for the people involved. As you will agree, extreme emotional or psychological dependence in an interpersonal relationship creates a morally ambiguous context for interacting with the other person. In the nation-state, however, political and economic dependence is thoroughly institutionalized. How can I hope to effect a consciousness of moral problems on the "state"? Only by influencing the individual officials of the "state." But, even were I able to influence a large number of government officials, the fact that each of them is in a position of extreme political interdependence with his constituents means that whatever choice the official makes in his official capacity he is making it not for himself alone, but for a number of other people whom he is supposed to represent. It is possible for one man to make some kinds of choices in a representative fashion for other people, but the moral choice is not one of these. Morality derives from the individual's responsibility to bear the consequences of his own choice. How can one man presume to burden others with the consequences of his own choice?

(3) Point 2 is based on the assumption that if nations have morality, this morality derives from the cumulative individual morality of the members of that nation. Under this assumption, we must say that if two men (a nation) make contradictory choices in the same situation, then the cumulative moral choice

of the two men taken together is neutral. Or, if three men (a nation) make two choices, one by two and one by one, the choice made by the two men represents the cumulative morality of the three men, taken together. The contradiction which thus arises (and this case is simple in the extreme — imagine 50 men making 30 mutual contradictory moral choices!) is the same as before: A man is burdened with the consequences of a choice which he did not make.

(4) Suppose that the definition of a nation's morality is different from that given in (3). Can you think of another definition?

Democracy is good, but it is not necessarily moral — in fact, it is amoral. Morality is a matter of the individual conscience. It cannot be decided by a majority vote; it cannot be legislated. Enough of this. You should try to read Niebuhr. He explains why "collective morality" cannot be the same as the morality of the individual. . . .

T.

January 29, 1968

Darling —

. . . I am concerned with two conflicting goals in my intellectual pursuit of enlightenment — one is the presentation and defense of my personal commitment, a commitment which is at least partly existential and therefore cannot be defined by pure "reason" alone; the other is to discover, through interaction with other people, what may be the common denominator in all men's commitments, i.e., the "truth" of human commitment. The problem — the conflict — in this dual aim can be simply illustrated . . . by consideration of an athlete's attitude in a contest. On the one hand, he hopes and strives to win for the sake of his own satisfaction — for the sake of the commitment in time and energy which he has made; on the other hand, his love and respect for the game — his sense of sportmanship — compels him to hope sincerely that the "best man" may win. Both elements of his attitude are essential to his integrity as an athlete; without the first, any contest, any test of skill — of commitment — becomes a sham. (Is it clear why this is so?) Without the second, the contest loses its meaning in the overall terms of the game. If the contestants play only to win, by any means and at any cost, they are not really playing the game at all but are merely using the context of the game in order to assert personal ambitions. . . .

. . . If we may be permitted to make the rather overused metaphor serve our purpose, then the translation of these attitudes of the athlete into the broader context of "the game of life," in which we are all contestants, is useful. (I am intrigued with the parallel because it is imperfect — in life, not only do we not know precisely what the rules are or what exactly constitutes "winning," we are also unaware of the real significance of the contest.)

T.

February 1, 1968

Toni —

. . . It occurs to me that one of the great dangers of the New Morality (not by intention, perhaps, but by implication) is that people will think that moral decisions — choices — are somehow "easier" than under the old law-morality. To the contrary, they are much more difficult because only under a morality like that proposed by the New Moralists is authentic choice possible. Moral decision under law-morality does not involve real choice at all — except the choice between what is "obviously right" and "obviously wrong." Now we are faced with no such absurdity — rather, we are asked not simply to choose the right or the wrong action, but to decide fundamentally and situationally what constitutes "rightness" and "wrongness" . . . .

T.

Princess —

There is an important dialogue going on these days between some writers and theologians. For instance, most (many? some?) students are familiar with T. S. Eliot, but they think of him almost exclusively as a writer of weird and beautiful poetry whose main value is existential, i.e., description and analysis of the human condition. But Eliot's poetry answers very few questions it raises. Eliot is an orthodox Episcopalian — a fact which most students note by way of a footnote. But it is only in the context of Eliot's religious faith that one can fully understand his poetry. As Tillich says: ". . . the Existentialist raises the question and analyzes the human situation to which the theologian can then give the answer, an answer given not from the question but from somewhere else and not from the human situation itself." You don't have to agree with Tillich, nor with theologians in general, but you do have to acknowledge their existence and significance. . . .

. . . I am just about fed up with militarism. I mean, I am angry. People want to fight wars? All right — go ahead. See where it gets you. Never mind the innocent people who have their homes destroyed, who lose their families, who get killed. Never mind the enemy soldiers — kill them, execute them, torture them. He's never done anything to you, but his leaders and your leaders don't like each other. Very good. Kill, kill, kill. Soldiers kill and citizens hate. Just jolly, World. I love you. God. Of all the incredible nonsense! Dear and glorious leaders of the world! Listen to me. Be gentle. Be human. You're driving me crazy. God. Frustration plus. I feel like giving up. Stop. Hold on.

T.

Sunday 2.4.68

Judy —

. . . The idea that everybody has to study the same thing in the same way is one of the worst prejudices in the public school system. You will encounter it again and again in high school and college; I don't think you can change it — at least, not while you're a mere student. But you can refuse to go along with it if you are sure that your own way is better *and* that you are willing to accept the consequences. You should never reject something blindly — always be sure that you can put up with the consequences. *Always!*

Love and peace,
Tim

5 February, 1968

Dear parents —

. . . I got a letter from Judy yesterday. The next four years are going to be rough for her — until she rediscovers her freedom and individuality in college. I wish I could be closer to her now. I feel as though I could somehow relive those terrible years vicariously through her and maybe help her avoid some of the frustration and despair. But maybe it's better this way. Otherwise I'd be tempted to restrict her own independence in the name of well-meaning advice. . . .

You should tell Richard that he can write to me any time he feels like it. Richard — are you listening? — how is your basketball team doing? I'm sorry to hear that you have the German measles, but that's what you get for having a name like Zimmer. . . .

Love and peace,
Tim

2.6.68

Dear Richard —

. . . I am working in the laboratory of the hospital now. The most interesting work I do is with blood and bacteria. . . . By

the way, your mouth contains about 186,000,000,000,000,000,000,-
000 bacteria. That's why it's important to brush your teeth. Be
happy.

Love and peace,
Tim

Wednesday 2.7.68

Father —

. . . Dick Krajeski came to see me today. We had a very stim-
ulating discussion of some aspects of contemporary Protestant
theology. Dick is an empiricist and existentialist — he doesn't go
along with Tillich's ontological approach, though he does admit
some value in the idea of "ultimate concern." I have a few
questions about that myself. How does one measure the ultimacy
of concern? Does everyone necessarily have an ultimate concern?
Does it make a difference whether one realizes consciously the
nature and implications of his ultimate concern? Indeed, is it
possible to speak of an ultimate concern which is unrealized by
the self? Dick is much more comfortable with Karl Barth, so I
am going to try to read some of his works. He also talked about
his own feelings about Christian faith and the church. They
were so startling to me — and, I think, to him — that I haven't
fully absorbed the implications. I intuitively feel that what he
said about the existential character of the choice of faith is
extremely important, but I'll have to think about it some more.
He suggested, for instance, that his true function as a minister is
to present his congregation with the bare-faced choice between
being a Christian and being other than a Christian. If there is
to be a transformation and revitalization of the church in our
society, it seems to me that it must come about through this
direct, unequivocal challenge. Christianity suffers, I think, from
being in favor, in the majority. . . .

I am still reading Tillich, and despite Krajeski's criticism I
am still intrigued with him.

Love and peace,
Tim

Darling —

. . . Putting my anger away so that it comes out in headaches is not conscious. At worst it is a habit which works subconsciously, but it may be a transformation process which takes place so deep in my subconscious that it is beyond habit. I rarely feel anger — I mean, almost never. Anger at distant, abstract things, yes. But the immediate and concrete are too many-sided for a simplistic reaction like anger. Let me say it this way: To you, whom I know and love as myself, I can show my anger; I trust you; I can show you the single isolated aspect of me which is my anger because you will be able to understand it as a part of me, whom you know. There are few people whom I love and trust as I love and trust you. To the rest, to show only the simple side of anger would be dishonest, for they will not understand it as it is in me. They do not know me well enough to understand my anger, so I conceal it from them, not consciously, but spontaneously because the realization of our mutual estrangement is spontaneous, instantaneous. . . .

When you get mad, you are defending yourself against the demands of reality. God keep our outrage. And it can be — it has to be — a legitimate defense unless it becomes permanent; at that crucial point, "getting mad" changes to "becoming mad." A defense against the harsh demands becomes a total surrender to the power of reality. Understanding is the only consistently effective weapon against the demands of reality. There is constant tension between reality and the mind's perception — either "passive perception" or "active vision" — of reality. It is the mind, not reality, which is the underdog; and it is the mind which can use the special weapons of madness or understanding to resolve the tension. Understanding consistent but limited madness, a brief purging of the soul of its anguish, is indispensable. . . .

. . . Do you really understand why I am here? If you don't, if your doubts are more than just doubts, we'd better talk about it. I told you once that I feel guilty, not about what I have done, but about some of the consequences of what I have done — being separated from you, from my family, from society. The fact that I think it was necessary, morally, does little to assuage my guilt — only your understanding can do that. But it must be your understanding, full of doubts, and not some counterfeit of certainty. . . .

T.

Thursday 2.8.68

Judy —

... When you get to college you'll be ready to learn the things which you should learn in college instead of having to catch up with yourself. ...

Love and peace,
Tim

Thursday 2.8.68

Darling —

... Marriage is not a prison — it is precisely the opposite of prison. Marriage means accepting responsibility — ultimate and lifelong responsibility for Toni — whereas prison is the complete denial of personal responsibility. Technical responsibility, the responsibility and concern for things, is an important element of prison life; but existential responsibility — the liberating concern of one human being for another — is possible only in free life, and in marriage. To be bound to a person by love for life is not any form of imprisonment; it is the utter freedom of self-fulfillment. I could never be free without you, Toni. You know that. You have to know that. I will exist only in potential until I am with you in marriage. To exist only in potential, without actuality — that is prison. ...

... Vietnam, Cambodia, and Laos have strong geographical and ethnic ties; if it weren't for the good old U.S.A., they might have found an effective buffer against any Chinese pretensions (or intentions) in the South. I am convinced, despite L.B.J. and Dean Rusk, that the Laotians and Cambodians know what is best for themselves; the U.S. is just one big nuisance. North Vietnam can never become to S. E. Asia what the Soviet Union was to Eastern Europe (but is no more). North Vietnam, assuming that it is still around for the next few years, simply isn't in any position, economically, temperamentally, or politically, to dominate her neighbors. I think that a partnership among equals — Laos, Cambodia, and Vietnam — is the most realistic possibility. Another alternative, the basis of the "domino" hy-

69

pothesis, is that China will assume the role which Russia assumed in Europe during the 1940's — the *enfant terrible*. I think such a possibility is supportable only in a simplistic context of historical transposition. China is not now what Russia was; S. E. Asia is not what Eastern Europe was; the world situation is not now what it was in 1945. The main factors which are preventing China from a Stalinist role in Asia are: (1) the existence of Russia, (2) the anti-colonialist nationalism of S. E. Asian peoples, (3) the fact that World War II ended more than twenty years ago, and, of course, (4) the good old U.S.A. However, point (4) is rapidly depleting point (2) of its significance. China did not introduce troops into North Korea until MacArthur was practically on the banks of the Yalu; and China hasn't yet introduced troops into Vietnam, even though the U.S. is bombing targets within a hundred miles of the Chinese border. But, the U.S. is pushing its luck. Before the escalation of the war in 1965, the chance that China would directly and materially dominate S. E. Asia was so slim as to be negligible; in 1956, the possibility was, despite American hysteria to the contrary, nil. Now, if the U.S. destroys Vietnam, which is a rather frighteningly likely possibility, a confrontation with China will become inevitable; and the U.S. will be forced to annihilate the most populous, most unfortunate country on earth.

Korea, North and South, is in a slightly different position from Laos and Cambodia. But it would be so absurdly easy for the North Koreans to make Korea another Vietnam, that the difference may be a matter of a few months. North Korea has not done anything really significant so far. For what reasons, I don't know. But they are certainly showing more restraint than the U.S. is showing in Vietnam.

How do these situations affect President Johnson's peace effort? I am sure that L.B.J. wants peace, but he wants it on his own terms and that is not only impossible but totally unrealistic. The fact that I have an argument with the Administration about America's *intentions* in Asia derives from a very basic difference of opinion; but it doesn't take a pacifist or revolutionary to see that disaster is disaster no matter how good or bad the intentions behind it. Even if I supported American aims in principle, I could not condone the way the war is being fought by any means. The significance of Korea is largely a matter of unpredictable contingencies: the Korean situation could become directly pertinent *if* North Korea does this or that. The problem deserves serious study. Laos and Cambodia are more important, rather, they could be more important if the U.S. would realize their legitimate claim to importance. If the U.S. continues its course in Vietnam, the chances are that the potential importance of these two countries will disappear entirely — they will become as totally dependent on the U.S. as Saigon is now. L.B.J. may not want to doom the U.S. to a permanent commitment, militarily and politically, in S. E. Asia; but doom does not listen to men's intentions but derives from their acts, and the U.S. is dooming itself by its actions to a colonial policy which will break the back of American freedom.

T.

Thursday 2.8.68

Mother —

... I have to confess that I have been neglecting physical exercise almost completely. Perhaps with the return of nice weather and the opening of the recreation yard, I'll be better about it. I can't tolerate the gym here; it was built to serve fifty people at most, but there are five hundred inmates here and far more than fifty of them use the gym. Anyway, I am far too busy. I spend most of my evenings writing letters and studying — my reading has fallen off drastically. But I am occupied, and oblivious to the desultory aspects of my environment. (I'm having trouble with words tonight.)

I guess what I'm doing is *just* surviving — I can manage it for a while, but not forever. . . .

Love and Peace,
Tim

71

Toni —

. . . it's a big world. There is plenty of room for all kinds of people, activists included. I am not by temperament an activist; activism involves a sacrifice of individual personalities really. I would only assume an activist role under the most pressing necessity, if I thought I could bring to bear an influence of respect for individuals where it is sorely needed. Activism has the same dangers whether it is in the context of the military (I don't mean peace activists in the army, but soldiers, patriots. Soldiering is the most common form of activism.) or the peace movement. T.

Sunday 2.11.68

Judy—

. . . I got your letter, which was enclosed with one from Dad, yesterday.

I think I know what you mean when you express your doubts about your true personality and your own value as a person. . . . A person's value as a person is not discovered in himself alone, but in his relationships with others. That's one aspect. But it is also true that a person's true personality resides almost entirely within himself; it is his own most precious, most personal possession. That is another aspect. Life is largely the result of the tension between these two poles of being: your life in and through others, and your life in yourself. You have to find your own way to deal with the tension, for I think that you will never be able to resolve it completely.

I do believe this: that what others think of you is not half so important as what you think of yourself. To act merely to please another person (and you can never please everybody) is dishonest. You will have to learn something which is very difficult to accept — to be yourself. And if you're not sure what yourself is, it is better to act as you honestly feel than to pretend to be something you don't feel, merely to gain someone's approval. There is a difference between acceptance and approval. I try to accept every person I meet for what he is — I don't try to disguise him in my mind to make him more easy to take; that, I think, is the only way one can hope to come to love and understand all the different kinds of people that are in the world. . . .

Don't worry so much about what other people think. After all, until you show them what you really are, anything they may think would be irrelevant. Some of my best friends — here and at school — are people whose ideas and life-styles I can't even comprehend, let alone approve. But I accept them and they accept me — mutual understanding will come, mutual approval is not really important. Don't be afraid of people — but if they seem to reject you, don't compound the rejection by returning it — do unto others as you would have them do unto you.

Love and Peace,
Tim

Monday, 12th February, 1968

Darling —

The problem of activism troubles me personally. It is apparent to me that a truly human relationship can exist only at the level of the I — Thou; that is, in the context of an individual's meeting another individual. Any attempt to "structure," organize, or institutionalize human energy, the human spirit, leads to a progressive dehumanization — rather, to be quite fair, to a strong tendency toward progressive dehumanization — of the interpersonal relationships which are characteristic of the organization or institution. Relationships between persons come to be no longer "interpersonal" but rather "intercategorical" — the potential I — Thou becomes I — It, or as I prefer it, It — It.

The dehumanization of human relationships is apparently unavoidable in our society and is not, in itself, a positive tyranny over the human spirit. Rather, it is at best a nothingness, a holding in abeyance of the individual's creative capacity, which, if it persists in all aspects of one's life, will lead to atrophy and stagnation. However, in reality, the nothingness is never absolute, nor does the tendency toward dehumanization maintain a consistently passive character. Every human being, at some point in his life and to a greater or lesser degree, experiences an essentially human meeting with another person. This I believe because no matter how dehumanized one's situation may become, the element of humanity persists and indeed is at the core of one's being. "Dehumanization" itself requires the existence of the human element in order to have meaning. On the other hand, the emptiness of categorized being does not remain empty for long in a social context; the ethos of categories fills the emptiness where human love is unable to fulfill itself; passive nothingness becomes the something of It — It. This is positive tyranny; this is the divorce of man from his essence, from his identity. A man is a man — nothing less. When he is considered as less, as an object, as a cog, as an enemy, as an ally, he is taken from himself. The consequences of this divorce are the ontological crises of identity in modern man and his inability to meet others as human beings.

Activism has, as a necessary precondition, the dehumanization of human relationships. That is to say, an activist is required to resort to categorizations because the problems which he hopes to resolve can only be conceived in terms of categories. Freedom, justice, fairness — these are categories. As concepts they are unnecessary to, indeed are inimical to, truly human I — Thou relationships.

However, the categories which the activist concerns himself with are derived from very concrete human needs and agonies. These needs and agonies exist for large numbers of people. How is one to respond to them? There are several practical alternatives: indifference, based on self-willed ignorance; concern, which humanizes but does not help; activism, which dehumanizes but may help. I guess what I want to be is an activist without the ethos of categories; a revolutionary of love. Impossible maybe.

T.

Monday, 12th February, 1968

Judy —

. . . I hope your schoolwork is interesting. Mine is not. I miss the classroom — the professor and the other students. I used to

74

feel, when I was in high school, that I would do better on my own — I still think there was some truth in the feeling. But college is different — the stimulation of ideas comes alive only in discussions. Your own thoughts become mature enough to be shared in a forum of peers; they become so important that they demand to be tested against the minds and convictions of others; and they become so large, so awesome that only life is a big enough textbook to contain them. In a sense, true maturity comes with one's commitment to a coherent set of principles, a life-style. In this you have not found yourself, but you have at least discovered the general terms through which you will hopefully be able to define and understand your true self. The essence of commitment is constant self-doubt, creative self-doubt. The child asks, "Who am I?" and gets no answer. A person on the verge of maturity asks the same question; he too gets no answer. Instead, he answers himself, "I know not who I am, but this is what I can become." Until the answer comes — and I'm not sure that it ever does come — there is doubt.

Love and peace,
Tim

Tuesday, 13th February

Mother —

. . . The March issue of *Esquire* contains a remarkable article on the subteen subculture in some segments of American society. Rather disconcerting, the first generation of the Marshall McLuhan era. . . . This generation of college students may already be an obsolete, a passing and rather pointless phenomenon. The thought frightens me. Between the tribalism of the primitive eras and the super-tribalism of the electronic age, a brief spark of individualism. Pfutt! I shall very probably find myself as a staunch, never-say-die defender of the conservative, verbal establishment, the linear thought school. Television is all right, computers have their purposes — but my conception of human values is rooted in the individual and culturally in the written word. I feel that I shall probably be fighting a losing battle

75

against the inexorable tide of progress and history. Programmed personalities may seem like an Orwellian fantasy, but fifty years from now, when my children's children marry, they will be accomplished, if unintended, reality.

Ah, well, perhaps the sands of time will sift so slowly as to be imperceptible. Notice, though, the magnificent optimism implicit in my forecast — I am assuming that the trend will be toward electronic tribalism without a sudden and violent regression to primitive tribalism.

Love and peace,
Tim

Monday, 26th February, 1968

Princess —

The war news is depressing. We are getting in so far that the whole problem is being distorted. Formerly, if one opposed LBJ's policy in Vietnam, it usually meant that one was opposed to war; today, opposition to the war policy is just as likely to be hawkish as dovish. People — officers — hear the news of reserve call-up; they're shook; for the first time they begin to re-think the war; they conceive alternatives not in terms of war or no war, but limited war or total war; they decide that the war should be drastically escalated. Maybe Eliot was wrong — not with a whimper, but a bang.

The real test of a pacifist's convictions will come in a time of sharply escalated hostility. As long as things are going fairly well "over there," people, generally, could afford to be tolerant. But when the situation begins to look bad for our side, the dialogue suddenly shifts locus. Truly, when we are up to our neck in quicksand, "my country, right or wrong" will be the watchword of the citizen. The citizen can pay lip service to truth and justice in times of milk and honey; but when the milk sours and the honey flows no more, truth and justice are reviled, for they are enemies of irrationalism, emotionalism, fervent patriotism.

All this will happen within the next five years — I believe

this, so small is my faith in reason and cool-headedness of our leaders and the bulk of the citizenry. It will be tragic.

For the dissenter, there are several alternatives: compromise, tactically defensible, but unsound as a basis for decision-forming; withdrawal, the easy way out, ineffective, but perhaps justifiable *in extremis;* indifference. It is obvious to me that the best attitude is one which combines persistence and a kind of Stoic detachment.

T.

Saturday, 2nd March, 1968

Darling —

. . . Cox's *Secular City* is fascinating, challenging. I'm not sure that I agree with a lot of what Cox says; and then, when forced to admit that he's right, I'm not at all sure that I approve. One problem is that modern society is so complex, such a hodge-podge, that no categorical characterization of secular culture will be very accurate. Cox tends to play down the traditional ethical problems in secular society. For instance, he notes that a prevailing attitude of pragmatism can lead to an ethical assertion of the validity of ends over means. He says, however, that this doesn't have to happen, that it is merely a deviation, albeit a significant deviation, from the true function of pragmatism. Very well. But it does happen, too often in modern society, and its evils sometimes achieve such proportions that we are forced by conscience to abandon the study of the true nature of pragmatism in order to deal with the evil of end-oriented deviation. This is precisely what has happened in Vietnam. I am all for disciplined pragmatism which realizes that effectiveness is *a* measure of value only when the value itself is rooted in a wider conception of morality. Thus, if one wants to eliminate 6,000,000 Jews, there are more effective and less effective means which one can employ. But the best means, in this instance, is not good in a wider sense. Likewise, pragmatism must be means-oriented if it is not to become utilitarianism. There is no such thing as an end in itself. Means and ends must be considered as one complex

77

of demands to be dealt with as a single problem. For there is no end which may not be considered a means to another end, and likewise no means which may not be considered an end in itself. This is all a little shaky, but I think it can be defended. Ultimately, however, verification of this principle must be intuitive and existential rather than dialectical. Cox points out that one of the greatest ethical teachings of the New Testament is Christ's injunction to *do the truth* to people rather than merely speak it. . . .   T.

Wednesday, 28th February

Dear everybody —

Just a short note to tell you that I received the Parole Board's decision today. I go up again in January, 1969; not very encouraging, but about what I expected.

. . . Now that I know for sure how much longer I'll be here, I feel more confident about the immediate future. I'll have to set up a series of goals to help me get over the difficult period when Toni will be in France.

Love and peace,
Tim

Wednesday, 6th March, 1968

Darling —

Your letter today was depressing — the effect of the draft at Earlham. How many senior boys will graduate this year, their plans for graduate study blasted by the mass cancellation of graduate student deferments: four years of study, of intentional growth, of learning and teaching, questioning and appraising, planning and dreaming — all that for what? To offer — to surrender — their bodies, their expanding and critical minds up to a system of dehumanized brutality. A few will say no for various reasons. They will leave the country — or go to jail. The rest, the majority, will submit, not eagerly, perhaps not even willingly, but they will submit. They will be taught to kill — not people, but "the enemy." They will be taught to destroy — not homes and fields, but strategic military targets. They will be inculcated with hatred — not passionate, human hatred, which cannot be taught, but detached, reasonable hatred, the product of inhuman necessity, a demand of tactical considerations. These scholars, these artists, these teachers, these human beings will become numerical factors in estimates of troop strength, statistics in newspapers. They will surrender their wills to unquestionable authority; their capacity for responsibility will be restricted to limitations set by orders and commands. The universal soldier marches on — the universal soldier with a liberal education. The future will praise, history will note, these conscripted lovers of knowledge — for what they might have been.

T.

Tuesday, 12th March, 1968

Dear Judy,

. . . Letters really make a difference in prison. Some boys here almost never get any mail. They are really alone — and most of them have been alone all their lives. . . .

Love and peace,
Tim

Wednesday, 20th March, 1968

Judy —

. . . The Theater of the Absurd, of which Ionesco is an outstanding proponent, appeals to us in this age because it is essentially true to our predicament — conventional forms, traditional customs no longer have any meaning. The principal focus of many of the plays of Ionesco and Beckett is this meaninglessness — it is a negative, rather than an affirmative, theme. It is very well and necessary to portray the discrepancy between form and reality. But caricature is an easy way out — characterization is the true value of drama. Modern "absurd" drama is essentially caricature — there are a few exceptions. There is little real comprehension of positive values, of personalities. All this is not in itself objectionable — but it does mean that productions of absurd drama require less ability than do the more traditional plays. Perhaps that's all right, though. I don't know. . . .

Love and peace,
Tim

Tuesday, 26th March, 1968

Dear family —
Well, today marks the end of my eleventh month. That's something — not much, but something.
. . . Modern Israel fascinates me. I think I'm a *kibbutznik* at heart. Israeli militarism is no less reprehensible than American militarism, but the situation in Israel is so much more hopeful — I guess that sounds strange. Well, it is — strange but true. If I were an Israeli citizen, I'd probably be in prison for the same reason I'm in prison now. But I think I'd be happier there. Ah, idle speculation. . . .

Love and peace,
Tim

Thursday, 28th March, 1968

Mia Carissima Mater –
. . . I have read the *Look* article on Draft Board No. 13. All

moral prejudices aside, the draft system in this country is remarkably antediluvian and anti-democratic. It's almost fantastic and reminds me of civil administration in pre-Revolutionary France — everything so vague and arbitrary, so confusing and demoralizing. It would be positively hilarious if I could forget the faces — so intent and serious, so perplexed — of the young couple in the *Look* article.

. . . I have been going through a mild crisis recently. This place has led me to compromise too many things of value. I was on the verge of apathy, of not caring whether an action or attitude was human or gentle. I thought this might be necessary for survival. I was wrong. Without the question of humanness, survival is meaningless. "For what is a man profited, if he shall gain the whole world, and lose his own soul? or what shall a man give in exchange for his soul?" (Matthew 16:26). (I want you to know that it took me almost twenty minutes to find that passage. I hope you're appropriately grateful.) . . .

Love and peace,
Tim

Friday, 29th March, 1968

Love —

. . . In most situations of life, there is no clearcut balance between the internal compulsion of conscience and the external coercion of "necessity." Compromise is inevitable, but it is always essential to base one's decision on the demands and needs of conscience. One must adjust to "reality," to be sure; this is pragmatic — and there is nothing *prima facie* wrong with pragmatism. But what I see and fear so much in many instances is that people take "reality" — their own particular conception of reality — as the basis for ethical decisions. This is not pragmatism, but utilitarianism. Pragmatism may serve the end of an ideal, so long as it does not violate the ideal, but utilitarianism serves only itself. Ultimately there is an absolute difference between the observer and observed reality. Even under the most rigid conditions of scientific objectivity, the gap cannot be bridged. . . .

T.

Dear Judy —

I have put off writing to you for three days. I was disturbed by what you described in your last letter. How do you explain prejudice and hatred, fear and unreasoning bigotry? I don't know. Why should you value human dignity? Why should you love a man simply because he is human? I don't know. What should — what can — the individual do in the face of inexorable events? I don't know. There's a lot I don't know; there's a lot I can't explain.

Words are not important in themselves. To call a black person a "Nigger" or a "dirty Nigger" is to say more about yourself than about anyone else. It is not simply a matter of courtesy or decency — though courtesy or decency can be a beginning. There is a sickness deep in the soul of a bigot. His is such a common sickness in our society — in most societies — that it is considered an inevitable hazard, like the common cold. It is something which has to be accepted simply because it has been accepted for so long. We have gotten along as racists for so long now, what would be the point in changing? That is the argument. People don't want to change. They won't change willingly.

People cherish their bigotry. They protect it from argument and persuasion. Some people even need it desperately in order to maintain their self-image. But it is not so simple. People need to be accepted, to feel that they are approved by their group. I have known boys here who can run down the entire catalogue of derogatory epithets, from "Coon" to "Nigger," and they do it fervently, sincerely. But those same boys have no objection to talking with a black boy, playing baseball with him — as long as it is understood that privately he thinks all black boys are sub-human nothings. Also, I have one good friend who can spout all the Black Muslim cant from memory — from not eating pork to killing all the white people. And he sounds fervent, sincere. But he doesn't mind talking with me, and I don't mind talking with him, even though he swears that someday he's going to kill me and all my white brothers. Why all these words? What do they mean? Are they just nonsense? No, not just nonsense. You have to look beyond the words to the feelings — and the feelings are the darkest and most suffocating in the human soul: fear, resentment, frustration, confusion. The problem is not that men are evil, but that they have no identity, no meaning. This means a vacuum, and as a vacuum is not selective, it does not evaluate or judge what rushes in to fill it. Empty souls are filled with all the stuff of unreason. Fear, bigotry, hatred — the debris which fills the vacuum.

The greatest tragedy is bigotry in children. Children are not afraid — they have to be taught fear. Children do not hate — they have to be taught hatred. Children are color-blind — they have to be taught that a black skin marks a person as despicable. All the reasons, the cant of bigotry, come later — they are adult rationalizations. Our only hope seems to lie in the children. What is the world coming to? Not to an end, Judy. That would be too easy. We have to live — not because it is good, but because we are doomed to it. The end of the world would solve all our problems for us. No such luck.

Love and peace,
Tim

Monday, 1st April, 1968.

Cara Mia —

. . . Well, Johnson's speech last night was quite something. It stunned me completely for half an hour. Things will have to be reevaluated. Right now I think McCarthy is my man. I'd vote for Kennedy, and Kennedy may be the best bet politically. But I think McCarthy is more trustworthy and more competent than Kennedy. Perhaps not. What do you think? You're still for Kennedy I think. I love you. . . .

. . . Johnson's decision was both brilliant and, I think, noble. His rather ambiguous de-escalation of the war was disappointing to me. First he halts the bombing — very well. You and I and McCarthy and Kennedy and the New Left helped to bring that about — Johnson took a difficult and very generous step. Then what does he do? 13,500 troops and 5 billion dollars — what is Uncle Ho to think? I hope, I pray — that Hanoi will reciprocate. The Vietcong are another matter. But frankly, I wouldn't blame the North Vietnamese if they were to do exactly what the Administration has said they would do during a bombing halt. This is a chance, a very slim chance, for things to change. I am hopeful but pessimistic. . . . My being in prison during this particular election year amounts to a personal tragedy. I want so much to be in the midst of political life. . . .

T.

Tuesday, 2nd April, 1968

Judy —

I got your letter Sunday, but I've been so busy and tired that I am only now getting around to writing you.

So, your first date. That's something. Do you mind if I feel a little jealous? Your first date. My goodness. I remember my first date. It took me a long time to get my courage up. In fact, it wasn't really me who did it. You see, I wanted to ask Kate to go to a movie. So I called her house, but she wasn't there. So I left a message, asking her to call me. She did. The house was full of people — a party or something. I was mortified. At first I refused to go near the phone. But mother more or less solved the problem by picking me up by the scruff of my neck and carrying me to it. I wonder to this day what Kate must have thought of me — I was tense; I couldn't say two words straight. As soon as she said yes, I murmured a curt "good" and hung up. But it was a wonderful evening, even though we had both seen the movie before. I hope your first date goes well. . . .

Love and Peace,
Tim

Wednesday, 3rd April, 1968

Darling —

. . . The secret to getting through prison days is to do things slowly, methodically. Don't rush. Don't take shortcuts. There's no hurry. Everything in its own time. Boredom is the enemy. Boredom is a state of mind, not a state of being. One can be bored even with a pile of work to do. To have nothing to do is not necessarily a reflection of objective circumstances. . . .

T.

Thursday, 4th April, 1968

Darling —

It's late. I've just come back from the hospital after patching up a thumb. Martin Luther King has been shot. He is in critical condition in a hospital. It's terrible. Tragic. I feel lost. My one American hero. He *has* to live. He *has* to. Toni, what are we to do? Things fall apart; the center will not hold. Is it too much to expect us, his brothers — black and white — to react to this senselessness as he would want us to, with reason, love, compassion? . . . He's dead. Good-night. He's dead. Dead. Dead.

T.

Saturday, 6th April, 1968

Darling —

. . . Martin Luther King's death has had a rather interesting effect on some of the people here. He was — is — greatly admired for entirely the wrong reasons by "moderates." It disturbs me very much but perhaps his death will help to make his dream possible. He was a great man, but one whose death has nothing to do with his true greatness. That he should have died for "his cause," and that he should be admired for that, is a travesty of his real meaning. He lived for men, for humanity; he worked for his people black and white. His death was a tragedy — a senseless accident. Nothing more or less. He should have lived. We need him now. We have lost more by his death than we have gained by the example of his life, brought to our consciousness through his death. I am not resigned, I cannot accept. His death will not save us. Only we can do that, and it would have been far better had he lived.

I feel lost. History has shifted into a higher gear during the past few weeks; too much has happened in so little time. The mind whirls, impotently, uncomprehendingly. We have sailed, in our small fragile craft of consciousness and experience, into a hurricane; the instruments of our comprehension are useless. How we long for smooth sailing, calm waters! Yet we feed the storm, agitate the waters, with our willful indifference. I have little use for those who praise Dr. King — words, shallow hypocrisy. Great men are not great for their words, and we do not approach, we do not comprehend, their greatness through words. No matter what men say, no matter what praise they mouth, unless they desire justice with their actions and manifest the spirit of nonviolence in their lives, their words and praises are less than nothing to me. Martin Luther King was a great man — why must men corrupt that greatness with meaningless words? The greatest tribute one could pay to Dr. King would be to remain silent — let the questioning, the searching confine itself to the heart. Toni, I feel so lost. . . .

. . . The world is either mad or apathetic — I'm not sure which is worse. It's interesting, though, that the anticipation of a catastrophe is usually worse than a catastrophe — the former can drive us to madness, the latter we either survive or don't. Morbid anticipation is a last resort — but what else can I do? I feel utterly powerless. . . .

T.

Tuesday, 9th April, 1968

Princess —

There was a short service in the Chapel this morning for King. An inadequate experience. Hymns and benedictions. I waited for somebody to say something meaningful — but the only people who weren't acting were the boys who sat behind me; they sniggered and cursed pretentiously during the entire service.

T.

Thursday, 11th April, 1968

Darling —

You're right about responsibility — we are responsible to other people. And yet each of us must be free to be private. There is a delicate balance. We must gauge carefully our capacity to accept the responsibilities of involvement — also the absolute responsibility to become involved. . . .

T.

Monday, 22nd April, 1968

Darling —

. . . I feel sort of lonely and friendless — a feeling which is mercifully short of self-pity. Reflection on the nature of existential anguish becomes a certain means of channeling obscure resentments away from one's own problems and miseries into more restrained, philosophical pessimism. I feel like that now. I need someone to talk with — someone older, who has survived youth; someone who speaks and understands my language; someone who will understand what I mean when I say that nothing seems to matter anymore; and finally, someone who will not belittle the anguish, the overwhelming vacuum of meaning which I perceive. . . . The thing about relating to people with or for whom you work is to imagine them in another context — at home usually. It helps put your own resentments and prejudices in a proper perspective when you realize that almost everybody cares for somebody somewhere. . . .

T.

Monday, 22nd April, 1968

Dear Mother —

. . . I didn't feel that Toni was particularly withdrawn last weekend. We were both feeling the imminence of her departure and so, I think, withdrew into ourselves. I think you are right that our relationship may subject Toni to unusual psychological strains. Under the conditions one could hardly expect it to be otherwise. The nature of our commitment to each other is distinctly anti-social in that it thrives on substance rather than form. If this is unfortunate because of external social drawbacks, then so be it — what we have found, what we hope to discover is somehow more relevant than social forms and psychological security (mediocrity). Life is risk — those are not mere words; they are the ruling principle of responsible freedom. We have together the strengths and weaknesses of two people who have somehow found in each other the compliment and fulfillment of their existences. Toni and I are inseparable — not in a physical or temporal sense — who can tell about that? — but in the sense that we have invested ourselves in each other to such an extent that that of each of us which is in the other cannot be neatly separated or distinguished. This is not mysticism; it is the most real fact. Everything I do is done for Toni — not because she does or would demand it, but because she is there when I do it. This all sounds a little silly, I'm sure. But I have never felt, or even imagined, such sublime confidence in a relationship with another person. . . .

I have been doing a good deal of writing — random speculations. About two hours a day. It is good and satisfying though I am afraid to reread what I have written.

Love and Peace,
Tim

Monday, 29th April, 1968

Dad —

. . . I really appreciated your visit yesterday. It was such a relief just to be with you alone for a while. I had been feeling very lonely recently. I miss my counselors and mentors. A continuous monologue with oneself becomes boring after a time. . . .

Love and Peace,
Tim

Monday, 6th May, 1968

Mother —

. . . I am getting along well with people here, learning more about myself as others see me. Not an invariably rewarding experience to be sure, but I have my good moments. I think I've finally come to accept the next year here. It's taken me a long time, but I have finally come to think of this place as my total environment — for a while. The less thought given to past and (present) future, the better. (That "present" was probably a Freudian slip of some kind!) I have made two new friendships here with boys who play tennis with me. A friendship is so fragile in the beginning. We glimpse the first thin threads of understanding which link us to others and are afraid to test them with the weight of our uncertainties. It is so long before we realize that only through such strain and tension do the threads become stronger. . . .

Love and Peace,
Tim

Wednesday, 15th May, 1968

Dearest Toni —

Things are not going well. This is about as bad as the situation has been since I have been here. Rumor has it that the honor dorms will be closed down next month, in which case I shall be going back to the dorm. Conditions there will be difficult. I have some hard, honest doubts that I shall be able to put up with life in the dorm, but we shall have to wait and see. I am very distraught at the moment and find it difficult to consider the situation in perspective. I feel very alone and isolated suddenly. Perhaps the rumor will prove unfounded; but that is not likely. Perhaps it will not be so difficult as I fear. At any rate, there is no use in crying over milk as yet unspilt. . . .

T.

Saturday, 18th May, 1968

Darling —

. . . It's becoming harder and harder to keep my spirits up. I find myself at secret war with my environment — hating the confinement, despising the people, resenting all the trivial, necessary activities of day-to-day existence. . . .

T.

Sunday, 14th June, '68

Dear family —

. . . I need other people desperately; without them life is winter and I hibernate. I need freedom too — freedom to choose and relate and move. Those who say they have achieved an inner freedom in the face of external imprisonment are speaking in a foreign tongue: what they have done is to transcend their imprisonment, their lack of freedom, freedom itself. They have not found freedom — they have gone beyond it and found something else within. I haven't done this; I don't think I would be able to; if I could, I'm not at all sure I would want to. I can accept my lack of freedom — its purpose and necessity; but I will never be able to reconcile myself to it. I rebel against it deep in my being and only through an exhausting exercise of will and reason am I able to avoid being consumed by the submerged rebellion. There will always be a critical ambiguity for me in society's attempt to deter lawlessness by imprisoning human beings. The most reprehensible criminal one may imagine — murderer, rapist, arsonist — still is human and preserves in his being something which I share with him and all men. Even when one makes a decision — as that to imprison a murderer — on the basis of reason and necessity (though we are never free of the spirit of revenge and simple degrading fear) the conflict is not resolved — the murderer (or any criminal) is still a human being, and this absolute transcends all other judgments on his behavior. This is an ambiguity and a contradiction which we must live with, I suppose. There is no way in which one can renounce his humanity unilaterally — this is perhaps where I

90

part company with the existentialists and find some corroboration in the Christian concept of the infinite mercy of God. In God's place I would put any man who is able, by a simple and irrational act of love, to encompass the despised and self-despised murderer within his own vision of humanity. Christ is in everyman to the extent that everyman can at some point commit the Godlike act of forgiving the unforgivable through love.

Perhaps I brood too much. I feel so useless, so at odds with myself. The ultimate rebellion for the individual would be the rebellion against the essential ambiguity of life — ultimate, not in the sense of being a shattering and apocalyptic denial of reality, but ultimate in the sense that it would be an end to reason and compassion. Many people rebel early in their lives and choose to ignore the contradictions of being. They become the Pharisees and Philistines of society.

Love & Peace,
Tim

P.S. Send money!!

24th June, 1968

Dear family —

All is well — don't be alarmed. This is just a friendly note to inaugurate my new keep-in-touch-with-the-loved-ones campaign. I have a schedule now which calls for five solid hours of serious studying and letter-writing a day. Tennis and bridge are just about out now since my partner in both will be leaving next month. . . .

Love and Peace,
Tim

Darling —

I guess you're wherever you were going to by now. You've been gone a week — that's 1/24 of your six months. Twenty-three weeks to go. Darling, I miss you miserably. I'm sure I miss you six months' worth already.

I got two postcards yesterday, from Iceland and Luxembourg. What a strange place to get a postcard from — Iceland. You are safe and happy. That's good.

The last week has been a critical period. Either I am going to waste the rest of my time here as I have the last ten days or I am going to shape up and stop vegetating. I am really trying to apply myself, but it's so hard. I feel very much alone and nothing seems worth the effort. I sleep a lot — too much — to escape idleness. I need so much to talk with you. I feel lost — not terrified, just perplexed. I need you.

I am going to try — for you for us. I can't let myself shrivel into a ball of subsisting daydreams. I love you, Toni. . . . I'm going to survive. . . . I love you. I do need you. I could live without you, but without you I don't think I could do anything at all. I love you, Toni. I feel better now. I should have written all this last week. . . . I can make it and I can make it worthwhile. All I need is a little of your strength and faith. I love you. Say hello to France for me. . . .

T.

Dear All —

Dick Krajeski visited yesterday. . . . We . . . talked about gun-control legislation and were unable to agree about anything specific. I feel about it rather as I felt about civil rights legislation a while ago: it will be ineffective by itself, a temporizing measure which avoids the real problem. It might be a good thing to have, but then too it might be totally useless. There are many sides to the issue and statutory oversimplification inevitably hinders rather than helps in resolution of such conflicts. Actually,

I find it hard to get excited about gun-control, having little use of the things myself. It does occur to me however that much resistance to any such legislation may arise from psychological feelings of being threatened sexually. What more ideal symbol of virility and potency than a gun? Gun-control — the emasculation of the American psyche. . .

Love and Peace,
Tim

Saturday, 29th June

Dear Judy —

. . . The problem of jealousy is one which you can never really solve by yourself because it always involves another person. It doesn't do any good to pretend that you are happy when you are feeling dissatisfied — it's dishonest in a way and it never really works because your irritation will come out in indirect ways if it is not expressed directly. The best way to solve the problem of jealousy is between friends. If the person of whom you are jealous is a good friend of yours, you should be able to say to him in a friendly way, "Boy, am I envious of you!" This solves two problems at once by bringing your friend into an active role in the conflict of jealousy which is otherwise purely subjective and internal. In this way you get the words out, you purge yourself of the secrecy and guilt of the emotion, if not of the emotion itself, and also you help the other person to express his feelings — for, remember that the other person probably realizes that you are uncomfortable or dissatisfied and this knowledge tends to make him uncomfortable too. . . .

It occurs to me though that how much money you make at an art fair is no way to judge the value of your work. Art — ideally — is the most anti-commercial of all activities because its finished products — paintings, novels, sculpture — have a uniquely intrinsic value which cannot be mass-produced but which, at the same time, is available to everyone for enjoyment. A best-selling novel is not necessarily because of that a great novel. Greatness in art lies in something other than salability. Maybe you would make a lousy merchant or manufacturer, but that's no great loss.

Love and Peace,
Tim

Thursday, 4th July, 1968

Darling —

It's Thursday afternoon — no work today because of the holiday. I've been outside today and have a fair-to-middling sunburn to prove it. My partner and I won the doubles tennis tournament. I ate four hamburgers and a hot dog at the picnic. So much for the holiday. . . . It's late Sunday night. My mother and father came down this weekend for a visit. I played golf with my father Saturday morning; he beat me and I really didn't do very well. We saw *The Fox* in Huntington — it is a fine movie, one of the best I remember seeing. Then we had a picnic in the park in Huntington. The weather was beautiful and the day was a success. I shouldn't say this, but I missed you terribly. I felt as though I weren't really there. I miss you always, but on visits it is worst. I love you. . . . How are things in Gallia? Have you changed? Do you think you will be radically transformed by this experience in another culture? It has happened. We'll have to get reacquainted all over again someday (it seems like years till January). I love you. You really should send me some good postcards so I can show all my friends what a world traveler my other self is. . . . Monday now. I love you. A letter today. I've upset you with my letter. Darling, you should never cry unless I'm there to comfort you and be gentle with you. Thinking of you being sad makes me feel all unsettled inside — a sucker for my woman's tears, that's what I am. I love you, darling. Please make everything you can of the next year. All I do now is wait — wait for you, for the future, for freedom. It's not a very creative or healthy state of mind. But it's only temporary — I know that someday we'll be together, free, in love. . . .

T.

Thursday, 11th July, 1968

Darling —

. . . Prison is not good. Its atmosphere is conducive to the dehumanization of inmates and officers. Mutual respect — not to speak of warmth — is the rare exception. There is something corrosive about the "system." Question: Is man basically good? If he is, why does he create and participate in the system which corrupts him? There seems to be something self-defeating about necessity: we do certain things (i.e., create systems) which we deem necessary to our survival, but then we become subject to the demands of what we create — demands which become gradually more divorced from the original demands of survival — and are changed by these demands until we are no longer what we had hoped to preserve, but are something else entirely whose raison d'etre derives not from the conditions of our original being, but from the created conditions of our corrupted being. A loss of innocence perhaps, but in the sense that we — man — are our own violators. We are corrupted not by the way things are, but by the way we have made things. . . . Friday evening now. The day was hectic. The operations started at nine and finished about 12:30. I was exhausted. I'm tired now. I love you. I miss you. This place is having a bad effect on me, I'm changing in perceptible degrees. I have become less patient with people — it takes an effort. It does no good to pretend patience when it isn't felt. It becomes condescension. The problem is that many people simply thrive on condescension. This is true — and unfortunate. Such a relationship is a civil, polite, self-perpetuating sham. Maybe I have some kind of complex. It's a problem, though. Most relationships are inadequate in very fundamental ways.

. . . Spock et al. were sentenced (2 years) and fined ($5000). The case will be appealed. Execution of sentence will be postponed for a while. I'm afraid this event is going to slip by largely unnoticed by the moderate middle class who, above all, should have been aroused by it. Spock made a fine call to resistance which will be heeded only by those who are already in the thick of resistance. Unless something really extraordinary happens — some flagrant violation of justice (flagrancy is relative — people become inured to progressively more flagrant injustices and build up a kind of moral resistance so that only progressively more flagrant injustices are capable of arousing them) — as I was saying, unless something really extraordinary happens,

I'm afraid we have missed the historical opportunity for meaningful and effective massive civil disobedience. It is strange that while our collective sense of awareness and vicarious participation has been vastly expanded through mass instantaneous communication, our capacity for effective action, our capacity for translating moral outrage into decisive political and social activity, has been stagnated and nearly paralyzed by the overwhelming vastness of the world which has been brought in its totality into confrontation with our senses. The escalation of awareness has been effectively cancelled out by the escalation of our capacity to tolerate the intolerable merely because it is too vast to be disputed. I'm wandering now. . . .

I got my first issue of the *Christian Science Monitor* yesterday. It is a good little newspaper, concise and unfrivolous though not immune to the prevailing political prejudices. The *Times* is still coming regularly, though my subscription has run out. . . . The *Monitor* today had a strongly worded editorial supporting the judge who tried Spock et al. Advocacy of illegal actions is not protected by the first amendment. Oh well. The problem is a little more complicated than that. The editorial did have the good grace to say a few good words for Dr. Spock however. . . .

T.

Monday, 22nd July, 1968

Darling —

. . . I spent yesterday with Dick Krajeski and his wife and daughter. Katie, their daughter, is 21 months old and absolutely the most charming little girl I have ever seen. She stole my heart, as the saying goes, and you'd better get back here right quick if you want it back! Dick and I went to church and heard an interesting sermon by Rev. Eiler. Then, in the afternoon, he, his wife, and I went to see *The Graduate* which was very good. Did you see it before you left? . . .

I really am trying to get various things done, like the diligent student that I am at heart, but I have come to the profound conclusion that my will to get things done increases in proportion as I am busy, and right now I am bored and lonely and get very little done. . . .

I had a letter from my mother today. She left Sunday for a Saul Alinsky convention on Social Action — it sounds very exciting. My father is somewhere in Kansas attending a conference on Draft Counseling sponsored by the Council of Churches. Judy has been participating in a drama workshop at Miami. Mother sent me the program which is very interesting. It includes bits and pieces from *Marat/Sade, The Deputy, Lysistrata,* and a series of readings of anti-war poems. These are high school students and, oddly enough, they seem to be encountering the kinds of ideas that high school students should but usually don't. . . . Ah yes, beginnings. Resolutions. One can never wipe the slate clean and go back to *the* beginning; but all successful change, it seems to me, comes from taking stock of what is on the slate and then making *a* beginning from that. I don't have in mind anything basic or fundamental or shattering; I'm in no condition for a reevaluation of my entire life-style; at any rate I don't feel the need for that kind of radical beginning. What I am thinking of is simply my day-to-day, hour-by-hour, task-by-task accommodation to the environment — my capacity for creative adaption (that's a good phrase) — or, more simply, making the most of things. To you I can with some degree of honesty confess my failures. I don't study diligently enough. Why? There is no immediate reward in it — I don't have teachers or fellow-students to argue with. I am not doing my work in the hospital as well as I should. Why? I'm bored; I'm a little bit lazy. The problem in both these respects is the lack of a reward. Except out of necessity, no person performs well except in pursuit of some form of reward. This varies from person to person and from task to task. For me, I think, the most motivating of rewards is that of contact and interaction with others. I don't mean praise or approval — these are, more often than not, merely alibis, excuses easily put forward by people to hide their indifference. Real interaction does not stop with a few words either of appreciation or denigration — in an odd way it transcends personalities, goes to the issue, to the problem, the performance, which then becomes the catalyst to deeper interpersonal interaction. (Is that redundant?) Do you see what I mean? It is good that we accept each other for what he is. But this is a universal imperative and is the first thing to be discarded when we really meet each other face to face. I am a human being, but I am also me. It would not be enough, for example, for you to love only the human being in me — you had to meet and love the me in me. There is a kind of residual respect in all men for the humanness of their fellows. At least lip service is given. But life doesn't really have any substance until and unless you get right down to individual people and their problems. This is really personal involvement and it is what I find very little of here. Enough. I've been running on. I love you. . . .

T.

Monday, 22nd July, 1968

Dear family —

. . . With the kind assistance of the Chaplain I arranged to spend yesterday, Sunday, with Dick Krajeski and his family. Dick and I attended the service at his church in the morning. Before that I sat in on a discussion session in the church basement. We heard a taped lecture, given by a social scientist at Union Theological Seminary, on the social implications of mind-control. The lecture was fascinating and I was only disappointed that the group didn't have more time to talk about it. The group itself was rather interesting in that it was composed entirely of elderly pillar-of-the-community types and high-school age people in their late teens — talk about a generation gap! They could have had one swinging discussion.

The sermon was given by Rev. Eiler; it was quite interesting and I am sure it disconcerted many of the middle-aged couples who bothered to listen. His topic was marriage, and his approach was startlingly direct and almost brutal. Dick said afterwards that he wouldn't have dared to preach such a sermon out of fear for his tenure.

We ate lunch at Dick's home — hamburgers and a delicious tuna-and-noodle salad. His wife is charming and their 21 month-old child, Katie, is adorable — this kid is so cute that I really regretted having to leave that afternoon. Dick and his wife and I went in to Ashland to see *The Graduate* in the afternoon. It had been held over by popular demand. The movie was very good, though not so memorable as *The Fox*. Movies really seem to have improved since I left the tender folds of the free. I got back to the institution about 4:30. Returning was a great let-down. It was a wonderful Sunday. . . .

Love and Peace,
Tim

Sunday, 28th July, 1968

Dear Family —

. . . About the New Left — that's kind of a deductive label. One doesn't join or choose to join the New Left. One simply becomes of the New Left if his attitudes and activities happen to coincide more or less with one or another segment of the wide range of attitudes and activities which are held to constitute the New Left ethos. . . . On the other hand, the New Left — the Movement — covers a lot of territory. It's impossible to define precisely since it has no very obvious formal structure. If a compulsion for self-criticism coupled with a vague loyalty-in-spite-of-everything is a criterion, then I'd say I am of the New Left. By the time I get out of here, it will be the criticism — not the ranting of the Right nor the tsk-tsk of the comfortably established moderates — which will be most essential. The pacifist is the inevitable critic in any political context, for the business of politics is power, whether positive (i.e., establishment) or negative (i.e., capacity for disruption), and the use of power against humanity is the definition, by contrast, of pacifism. Criticism is valid only when made with love — that is, criticism of life-styles. I find it easier to love the New Left critically than to love the establishment at all. . . .

Love and Peace,
Tim

6th August, 1968

Dear family —

... The Republican Convention is as dull as I had expected it to be. There is some potential for excitement — if Nixon misses on the first ballot and Rockefeller makes a strong showing. I don't think Rockefeller has much of a chance, but strange things have been known to happen.

It's interesting to note how things have changed since 1964. Then, it looked as though the GOP might be permanently split. Now it's the Democrats who seem to be in real danger.

Dad, do you remember our discussion of the possibility of McCarthy's running independently at the head of a fourth party? ... I would support McCarthy as an independent. As voters with a public conscience, we are faced not only with a choice between a greater and a lesser evil — we can, if we wish, choose between the present and the future. A politician, some one has said, is one who thinks about the next election; a statesman is one who thinks about the next generation. McCarthy is the only potential statesman in a prominent national position this year.

Love and Peace,
Tim

23rd August, 1968

Dear family —

... I have been deeply disturbed by the Soviet-led invasion of Czechoslovakia. It was a cynical and immoral international provocation comparable to Hitler's invasion of Europe and Russia and to the United States' present adventure in Vietnam. For the moment, it will provoke widespread aversion and censure on both sides of the Iron Curtain, but eventually the entire incident will find its due place in the normalcy of cold war politics — like Vietnam and the situation in the Middle East. The Czechs and the Vietnamese may prove to be the outstanding heroes of this decade, though this fame will little compensate for the futility of their attempts to resist political emasculation and physical depredation.

Love and peace,
Tim

25th August, 1968

Darling —

It's Sunday morning, the only time in the week when I am able to write letters. I am back in the dorm now and the combination of noise, confusion, heat, and flies makes concentration very difficult. I miss you much more than is good for me. My daydreaming is a continual and unsatisfactory groping toward the future — toward freedom and us together. . . .

T.

Thursday, 3rd September, 1968

Darling —

. . . I love you and I miss you and, the way things have been going lately, even if I didn't love you I'd probably miss you anyway. I'm trying to think of some way in which to tell you how vastly and deeply and inalterably I love you, but my mind boggles at the task. Numbers are in no way sufficient to the task because a number implies a comparison, and there is nothing of the same order which is comparable to my loving you. Poetry is nice, but it tends to defeat its own message by drawing attention to the poem as art.

. . . The closest approximation to my present state of mind which I can recall from the free world is the sense of utter peace I have sometimes experienced when I sat with you somewhere in the evening. Saying nothing, thinking of nothing, merely being aware of you and testing the bliss of our silent communication. Communion is better. Sometimes I sensed the full force of our remarkable oneness like a fire-hailed revelation, an irrefutable truth, acceptance of which is salvation and beatification and fulfillment. I love you. . . .

I had a fantastic dream as I slept this morning: I was living in a bungalow near a beach with my family. We were in the living room. I noticed a small, delicate brown bird wearing glasses and reading a book. As I approached it, the bird put down the book and glasses and proffered its wing, like a hand, and I shook it in greeting. The bird grew and became a young woman, her feet were bird claws. And the bird spoke to me and she said that she was the offspring of bird and brother and sister and that she was both male and female. A young man came in — he was dull and ugly. He also was both male and female. A doctor, a woman, examined them and found that they did indeed possess male and female characteristics. The doctor said that they were "Appodytes" — I remember the word clearly. I went back to school and there I met Kate and Janet. Each of them saw my friends — the bird-woman had human feet, she wore no shoes. She was looking for Paul Lacey, who was her advisor. I tried to explain to Kate and Janet about the bird-woman and the dull, ugly man. Janet got angry, saying that "appodyte" was a nasty word which no one ever says. She walked away in a huff. Kate just laughed and we went off to class. The class was one in journalism and the teacher was a strict and unsympathetic old woman who intimidated me. Everybody was to present his assignment, which, Kate explained, had been assigned the previous year. I was unprepared. That is all. I love you. . . .

T.

4th September, 1968

Darling —

. . . Nothing worth reporting has happened recently, so I'll bore you with a stream-of-consciousness list of the things I miss most in here: being with you, drinking beer in a crowded "bar" late at night, friends, arguing about literature and politics and history and science and religion, talking with you, browsing in bookstores, buying books, studying late at night, holding your hand and walking with you close to me, going to movies, going to cheap roadside restaurants, being gentle with you (which is, in all, merely being with you), playing touch-football, walking in autumn woods (this especially!), listening to you talk, listening to you breathe and listen, driving around in a car, lying on the ground and watching clouds, mowing the lawn, washing the dinner dishes with my brother and sisters, sitting in bus stations, walking at midnight by myself, reading in a library, buying a milk shake at the Dairy Queen, holding you close to me, going to a pizza parlor, walking, walking, walking, as though the earth were endless, making myself a snack late at night, touching your hair, your face, hearing your voice, sitting in tree-shade or in front of a fireplace with friends, going to strange, spontaneous parties with records and poetry and arguments, talking, talking, talking, being alone with myself, buying food for a picnic, buying cigarettes in a drugstore, feeling free. I love you. Darling, your letters mean more to me than anything else that happens to me here — including my visits with my family. Maybe I depend on you too much; but then, why shouldn't I? I love you. You are half of us — and us is the wave of the future. You and I, Toni, are going to conquer the world — metaphorically speaking. Of life I ask only two things: wisdom and Toni's love. All optimism and hyperbole aside, our marriage cannot help but be the happiest, most fulfilling, most exciting, most meaningful event ever experienced by mortal humans. I believe that with all the hard-headed practical sense I can muster. . . .

Archeology interests me more and more of late. There is nothing more exciting to me, even given all the hard, tedious work, the disappointments, and the limited chances of real success, than to rebuild a material picture of a lost civilization. I am, I think, infatuated with the present, but my true love is for the past.

. . . I feel very good. When I write to you, there is a bittersweet ache, like a pleasant memory charged with the future. I love you. . . . I indulge myself in daydreams, memories of the past and future us. When I come back to Earlham, you and I will walk around the campus and you will show me things that have changed, and I will remember for you things as they were. There is nothing inherently wrong with daydreaming; in healthy people it is a very healthy means of escape.

. . . My mother and I got into a rather tense argument about the movie, *The Graduate* on Monday. She objected to the characterization of Mrs. Robinson, which was not sympathetic; on the other hand, none of the characters was portrayed with any great sympathy, though this was more true of the adults than of their children. . . .

Be gentle
T.

7th September, 1968

Dear family —

. . . Mother — I have read the Alinsky material and have found most of it extremely interesting. Who is the author of *The Search for Certainty?* The best article was "Agitating Jesus." I'm going to ask the chaplain if he would like to read it. Alinsky fascinates me as a personality, though both his "philosophy" and his action program are not completely persuasive. His criticism of the traditional means-ends ethic is well taken, but is valid only if one retains the ethical structure and tries to improve it. Alinsky's ethical structure is no ethical structure at all, but a fairly lucid descriptive analysis of the way things are — that's science, not ethics.

Love and peace
Tim

8th September, 1968

Darling —

. . . I am someday going to write a profound and incisive essay about this experience entitled "Resignation and Resolution — Or, How to Live for the Future When You Can't Stand the Present." How about that? I love you. . . . People here upset me. Every once in a while, a group of inmates will gang up on a weaker boy and torment him nearly to despair. The victim's suffering bothers me, but not because of the suffering itself but because he, the victim, usually invites — begs for — the torment in order, perhaps, to fulfill some need of his own. What bothers me most, though, is the uninhibited pleasure — sadistic glee — the persecutors get out of their sport. Sadism is not normally manifest in human behavior, even among prison inmates, but it is latently inherent in human personalities. Cruelty depresses me — which is not healthy; it also angers me, which though "healthy," perhaps, is not rational. There can, I think, be such a thing as rational anger, anger used as a means toward certain human ends. But my anger toward sadistic behavior is neither rational nor healthy — it is of the same kind as the tense fury of the sadist. I am in a real bind. I love you, Toni. I need you desperately. How can I possibly solve these problems by myself? . . .

I have a little calendar on which I mark off the days as they pass. (Isn't that what a prisoner is supposed to spend his time doing?) Well, I do. I don't do it every night — that would make it a mechanical gesture; but every once in a while I look to see how long it's been since I marked off the days and I do it. Sometimes only two days, sometimes a whole week. . . .

We have so much that is new to learn, so much to do, so much to experience. The imagination staggers drunkenly in contemplation. I can now state categorically, and with the authority of experience, that prison life is not one of the better ways of spending one's time. I hope I shall never grow to hate this place; may we part as friends, like lovers who have grown tired of each other and recognize that they have nothing more to share. (And good riddance!) . . .

T.

Darling —

. . . Judge Porter sent me a copy of Abe Fortas's essay "On Dissent and Civil Disobedience." It is interesting and well done; however, I cannot escape the impression that these establishment liberals who express their sympathy with us nasty radicals as long as we don't go beyond certain limits of expression and behavior are being hypocritical. It's all very well to moralize against violence and hatred, but it is less credible when this moralizing springs from a prudent realization that *you* may be the victim of someone's frustrated hatred. In other words, it is a matter of saying the right thing for the wrong reason. Violence is wrong, hatred is deplorable — not because they destroy things or hurt people, but because they tend to be self-perpetuating. Fortas says that I, for instance, should do what my conscience demands, but must be willing to suffer the legal and social consequences — this I agree with, but it is a rather minor, ineffectual thing. To argue about the niceties of social intercourse while people are dying is an absurdity which nicely characterizes the dilemma of the affluent liberal. There is a contradiction in our society between the revolutionary aspirations of the radicals — both violent and nonviolent — and the concrete historical situation which is "rebellious" rather than revolutionary. . . .

Free life is going to come as a real shock for a while — imagine being able to do something you want to do without having to worry about returning to a cell when the day ends! Goodness. Will I be able to adapt? You're damned right I will.

I am growing to despise this place with most cordial intensity. . . . This place is, at best, a necessary evil. The philosophical implications of the statement — that evil can be necessary, that suffering is necessary — are provocative. I was thinking about the problem as I watched the movie tonight, and I came to the aphoristic conclusion that if there were no such thing as suffering, man would have to invent it. Quite so. Man cannot live without suffering, just as he cannot escape hope — the two are inseparable complements. The poles of human existence. But, and this is the vital question of all mythology (i.e., philosophy), which came first? I love you.

T.

Darling —

. . . I have long recognized, I think, that one of my great problems is that I don't trust people — that is, I have the greatest faith in their good intentions (which I value highly) but I am always doubtful of their ability to translate these intentions into good actions. Whether I am right or wrong in this mistrust is beside the point; my problem is that I worry too much about things for which I am not properly responsible. This is a psychological nuisance, but there is also a moral dimension to the problem: to feel responsible for another person's actions is a subtle form of condescension which poisons any relationship. Ideally, two people should meet in a relationship as equals — equals, that is, in the sense that they are equally free and equally responsible. This is not a mere pipe dream; in most relationships we can achieve this respect, each for the other's uniqueness. And this parity transcends all qualities of intellect and brawn, beauty and poise, wealth and social attainment. We are all, as individuals, different, and only in that respect are we the same. There are certain kinds of relationships which necessarily violate this ideal equality — parent-child, doctor-patient, jailer-prisoner. These we may accept as necessary, if not as necessarily evil. However, we have, all of us, at one time or another, experienced relationships in which we have felt mortally uncomfortable precisely because one of us — the I or the Thou — has abdicated his freedom and responsibility. In large-scale political terms, this abdication leads to fascism or dictatorship; in the more personal terms of human relationships, it is manifested in a self-reinforcing cycle of emotional dependence and dominance. There is nothing more frustrating or disturbing than such a relationship. At best it can be a pathetic swamp of deceptions; at worst, it destroys the very human qualities which make any relationship worthwhile in the first place. There is nothing more insidious than a "little" self-deception.

I encounter many people here who seem to be able to exist only as emotional dependents; in psychological jargon, one would probably say that they lack a sound sense of identity. This is not the same as the "identity crisis" with which I am more familiar, for the term "crisis" implies at least a struggle for an individual identity. The people I worry about are those who have given up (if indeed they had ever been given the opportunity to undertake) the search, the struggle, for identity. They are parasites and their tragedy is not that they cannot live without the emotional patronage of others, but that they can exist *only* in terms of that patronage. Ah, it seems that men can be like animals in more ways than one — the ferocious beast and the simpering puppy-dog are both beneath what we could be. . . .

Finally, my love for you engages me in the highest form of freedom — which is not freedom *from* responsibility, but is the freedom to accept full responsibility because I can be totally honest with you. Honesty, the freedom to be honest, is the liberating force which baptizes me in the freedom of responsibility. The freedom to be honest is the greatest freedom of all; it is the liberator of the human spirit. This is of utmost importance to me. It may be said, further, that self-honesty comes most effectively through honesty with others; that, in fact, he who gives his true self to others cannot be false to himself. I love you, darling Toni. . . .

T.

18th September, 1968

Dear family —

. . . Life goes on. I am reasonably content with the way things are going; perhaps I've finally descended into a stupor of indifference. No, that's not precisely the case. I've simply grown tired of futile worrying. There is an appealing if insidiously demeaning wisdom in that prayer: Dear God, give me the strength to change those things which can be changed, the patience to endure those things which cannot be changed, and the wisdom to know the difference. I am not at heart an activist. My commitment to a certain degree of activism comes as a duty concomitant to intellectual perception, rather than as an expression of my intuitive being. This fact does not, I think, detract from the quality of the commitment, though it may diminish its degree and effectiveness; at any rate, this peculiar quirk of my nature is beyond my power to change. Activism has its negative aspects, as well as its positive ones. But then, so does any chosen life-style. If we may speak of a personal truth, it is that quality in a person's life which is discovered as a result of living a commitment and which ultimately makes the life and the commitment worthwhile. Commitment, then, is the contemporary equivalent, in the necessary secular terms, of faith. Faith justifies itself and fulfills the life of faith. I cannot conceive a life without commitment, without its ultimate concern.

And yet, it would not do to deify commitment *per se*, to say, "It doesn't matter what you believe, as long as you believe something." I say this because there are commitments and ultimate concerns which strike me as inappropriate, but perhaps that is my fault.

Love and peace,
Tim

19th September, 1968

Darling —

. . . I have been having a few vivid and memorable dreams lately, and for the first time in many months you are in them again. It is interesting and a little disturbing that you appear in my dreams as an elusive, unresponsive figure: the you in my dreams is never there where I am, never feels the same feelings, never responds to the same things. The dream-you taunts me passively, indifferently. These dreams are most vividly associated in my mind with the times at school when I looked for you but couldn't find you. I experience, in my sleep, the same feelings of frustration and loneliness and (to be honest) jealousy that I remember experiencing then. . . . There is nothing more necessary to sanity which is more consistently violated by prison life than the need for privacy. Lacking happiness, privacy is even more imperative. I'm not anti-social. But there are times when I desperately need to be alone with myself. This sort of communal living in close quarters is repressive. There are no open fields or dark woods, no secret places. We are constantly rubbing our wounds against each other and there is no dignity in that. I used to think that the mind was sufficient refuge for the self in any situation; but that is a lie predicated on a rejection of the physical world. . . .

T.

29th September, 1968

Darling —

. . . The bureaucratic malaise is a chronic condition in this place. Disorder, sloppiness, just-getting-by are the normal circumstance. This is inherent in the philosophy of the institution, as it seems to be in government. Crisis upon crisis arises and is met according to the rules; little imagination, it seems to me, is expended by officials or inmates. The paramount consideration of security compels everyone here to cleave narrowly to the status quo. There is nothing which so stagnates an institution as a little success. . . .

Dick Krajeski was out to see me today. We talked about history and morality. Every time I talk with him I wonder afterwards why it is that I haven't gone absolutely stir-crazy in here. The absence of intellectual stimulation is so nearly complete that I can almost feel it as a huge vacuum. When I do have a chance to talk extensively with someone — as with Art Saturday or Dick today — I am utterly exhausted by the encounter (*not* because I talk too much but because I listen too absorbedly). I wonder how long it will take me to readjust to college when I go back. Quite accurately, intellectual deprivation is as debilitating as emotional or physical deprivation. . . .

T.

30th September, 1968

Dear family —

The weather is getting cooler, especially in the evenings. Soon the leaves will be turning and for a brief few weeks the hills beyond the fences will be a smear of colors. An autumn and a winter to go, and part of a spring. Seven more months, perhaps nine. I'm not sure now how I was able to face the prospect of three years in prison when I set the course two years ago. As I think of it now, there was a kind of anesthesia induced by the shock of commitment, a sort of numbing of the senses which apprehend the consequences of an action which is necessary because it is right. I think this is an appropriate comparison. How else to explain the courage and calm decision of the martyred? It wasn't courage at all, but a state of hypnosis induced by the conviction that what they were to do was right and true beyond any consideration of immediate consequences to themselves. That's very garbled. Oh well.

Love and peace
Tim

6th October, 1968
Darling —

. . . Dick Krajeski came out this afternoon and we listened to a taped lecture on the moral implications of scientific genetic control. It was extremely interesting. We — our age — may be on the verge of a tremendous revolution in man's ethical relation to the universe. Scientists are fast solving the problems of how to alter the universe to suit man's fancy, but we have almost no idea of how we are going to apply the solutions ethically. As I see the question, the matter hinges on Man's relationship with Nature. When Man, as he has been till recently, was largely subject to Nature, morality was an expression of his consciousness of this subjection: the Commandments were the words of God and they had to be obeyed because God (Nature) was a terrible and omnipotent judge. Now, however, as Man begins to play God more and more, the subjection is undermined and along with it the entire foundation of human morality. The implications are enormous. The very fact that we can now determine, to an ever greater extent, who shall live and who shall die, and that we shall eventually be able to determine how people will live and in fact what kind of people will be born, means that the responsibility for life and death will be shifted from God to Man. The political implications in themselves are staggering. What this development will mean for man as a moral creature is overwhelming. . . .

I miss you so much that I have moments of intense and irrational hatred for this place. I am utterly without communion or community, I think in my worst moments, and desolation is a disease endemic to my surroundings. All this jail bit is so foolish, so utterly without redeeming merits other than sheer necessity. Perhaps I am tied too much to you: there is no substitute, on any level whatsoever, for our being together. . . .

T.

Thursday, 17th October, 1968

Darling —

. . . There haven't been any great poets since Dylan Thomas — that is, poets writing in English. Many of the contemporary lot are competent and some are even good — but not great. I conclude this after reading more than eight hundred poems written by young (most of them under forty-five) poets during the past three decades. I have no particular favorites, though there are particular poems which I like. I feel somehow letdown. . . .

T.

Saturday, 26th October, 1968

Darling Toni —

. . . I'm in a doldrum now. It's not precisely a depression that I feel, but a vague sense of uneasiness. A lack of discipline. I can't keep at the things I should be doing. Nothing relieves the monotony. Monotony. Every day is like the one before, like the next one. Why should I do anything at all? What keeps me going is not any feeling that it's worthwhile; I simply refuse to surrender, to give up. "At worst, one is in motion; and at best,/ Reaching no absolute, in which to rest,/One is always nearer by not keeping still." [1] Is that enough? Floating. Drifting. I'm so tired. Nothing I do relates to anything. I feel irrelevant. There is so much I should do, so much I could do. And I'd feel much better if I would do it. But I feel as though I'm in a dream: my movements are slow and so heavy, nothing stays in its place, everything shifting, so tired, so hopeless. I'm afraid, scared into immobility. I should do something — write a letter, write an essay, write a poem. I should do it and be done with it. But I'm afraid — afraid that I won't be able to do it, to finish it. I'm afraid of the potentiality in my ambition. No, I'm not saying it. I'm afraid of my fear. What is it? What am I so afraid of? What? What? What? No distractions. Keep searching, asking. What? What? What is it I'm afraid of? What? Why don't I do all these things? Why? I will fail. I won't be able to finish what I've started. I won't be satisfied with it. It won't be worth . . . worth . . . worthy of me. Worthy of me. I'll fail myself. Miserable. Fail Toni. Fail Paul Lacey. Fail Judge Porter. Fail. Fail myself. It's closer. I'm getting there. Closer. I'm afraid that I won't be able . . . that I'm not good enough. Good enough for what? For me, for my potential. I'm wasting myself — that's the worst thing. How can I tolerate wasting myself? No. I'm getting off the track. I'll fail. I won't be able to do it — to say what I mean, to live what I believe, to create, to understand. Closer now. Fail fail fail. What? I won't be able to understand. I will fail to accomplish understanding. To complete, to finish, to understand. To create, express. Time. There's no time. I stumble over myself. Clarity. Clarity. Say what I mean. To accomplish. Fail to accomplish. I doubt myself. My intelligence. My capacity for understanding. So much to do. So little time. So much to do. Do all the things. Don't be distracted. Discipline yourself tim. Discipline. So tired. Discipline. So tired. Discipline. So tired. Concentrate. Accomplish. There is no such thing as perfect. No such thing. Perfection. No. No. No. I can do these things. I must not be afraid. No confidence. Give up. I can. I can. I will. I must. Everything. Discipline. Know what needs to be done.

[1] Thom Gunn, "On the Move," *Positives: Verses by Thom Gunn* (Chicago: University of Chicago Press, 1966) .

Don't give in. Work. Work. Priorities. Order. Know what you are doing. Don't be afraid. Nothing to fear but fear itself.

I don't dare read that over. Have you ever tried to psycho-analyze yourself? Exhausting. I feel a little better. Toni, do you trust me? Do you have faith in me? I need you. I need to believe in myself. I need time, alone, to think about things. I have none of the things I need. I need discipline. I need you. . . .

Now I recognize the fear; he's an old friend. The void, the emptiness of unaccomplishment. I *have* to do the things which will define me. I *have* to work. Single-mindedly. Keep at it. Only my own fear stops me. Help me, Toni. From thousands of miles of ocean and time, help me. I need you. . . .

T.

Sunday, 27th October

Dear Dad —

. . . Only ten days remain until the election. It still looks like Nixon all the way. I heard today that recent polls show Wallace's strength is falling off. From a purely partisan point of view I am relieved, but I don't agree with Humphrey that the real danger in Wallace's movement is that it threatens the two-party domination of politics. Given a cooler head and a less prejudiced outlook, even Wallace's presumptive constituency could constitute a valid force in American politics. That the two major parties fail to accomplish what needs to be done is an old familiar story; that they fail to represent every significant political minority is reprehensible — and also, perhaps, inevitable. Hence the weakness of the system.

I am getting along very well. I talked to an official earlier this week about my chances of being paroled in April or May of next year. He was sincerely noncommital; he said he simply didn't know. But I got the impression that he was basically pessimistic. I imagine that we'll just have to wait and see. Maybe a good letter from Judge Porter will help, though his letters in the past haven't had much effect. . . .

love and peace,
Tim

Darling —

... One of the recurring conflicts I experience — have experienced since I first became aware, in high school, of my intellectual identity (though at the time, in my budding egotism, it was my identity as an intellectual — a kind of retreat from and defense against a world which left me alone too much) — is the problem of being continuously relevant, of existing always in a kind of state of hyper-relevancy. Ideally, I disdain any activity which is not in some way meaningful. At worst, this leads me at times to involved or facile rationalizations concerning certain of my activities. For instance, playing tennis. Tennis is fun — and there's nothing wrong with fun — but I insist to myself that I "indulge" myself in it because the exercise is good for me (which is true enough also), and the benefit I derive from the exercise would not be diminished if I could persuade myself that I actually, in my deepest parts, play because of the fun. However, I do not so persuade myself, nor even try. And this applies to everything I do — even to reading novels; unless a novel is a classic, I don't feel comfortable when I read it, no matter how I enjoy it. . . . Fortunately, but sometimes also irritatingly, I am more complex than the sum of my aspirations and/or emulations. But in this case, knowledge of the problem does not appear to be half the solution. To be sure, I have been known to enjoy irrelevant activities simply because they were enjoyable — but when I recognize what is going on I immediately begin to rationalize. As far as I am concerned, my main problem is not my apparent inability to enjoy myself frivolously (I mostly enjoy myself in other things — study is very enjoyable, and our relationship, for instance, in its smallest aspect, is at once the epitome of relevancy and of joy), but that my constant efforts to justify myself in my frivolity require a considerable expenditure of emotional energy and spoil the fun besides. . . .

Incidentally, I've decided that I probably am fairly sane — well balanced in the essential core — which is something I've worried about for quite a while. Though rarely seriously. Maybe I'm just stronger than I thought I was. Or maybe I have only now wanted to believe and accept my own strength. My problem, I guess, is that I'm not very patient. Is that true? I wonder. I'm so confusing — hence confused. I love you.

The crux of the problem is that when people make statements about phenomena, the words they use (the names, categories) and values they apply have nothing to do, essentially or intrinsically, with the phenomena themselves, but with their own subjective feelings. It is only by consensus that we let these subjective criteria define and evaluate the objective phenomena. And this goes far deeper than moral relativity or selective justification. With respect to the essential nature of phenomena, a dogmatic and revelatory morality is not different from a relative or situational ethic. Even nihilism, since it is merely an ethic based on the accidental application of moral relativism, is no help. If this were the extent of it, if morality itself were not a phenomenon, we could deal with it by simply rejecting the possibility of detachment — since any detachment short of complete detachment is merely a degree of involvement. However, because we cannot escape from phenomena — our attempt to escape being merely another phenomenon — we are left with utter valuelessness, and love is hate, war is peace, life is death, right is wrong. In short, all things are the same. I love you.

T.

Friday, 1st November, 1968

Darling —

Let me tell you what's bothering me today. We heard a taped lecture on the population explosion. I'm sure you're at least vaguely familiar with the statistical horrors of current population growth, so I won't reiterate. The point is that either something rational has to be done or something irrational will happen. And whatever is to be done must be started within the next few years, almost immediately. There are two separate aspects of the problem which must be considered separately and simultaneously: the rate of population increase and the lag between food production and population growth.

Frankly, I've been distraught about the problem during the past few hours. What can any individual do? Where do we start?

First, in theory. If world population can be stabilized, beginning now, an all-out technological effort would be able to provide a minimum amount of food for everybody. But this depends on two big *if's: if* population growth can be curbed, and *if* an all-out technological effort to increase food production is made. The first if is solved quite simply in theory: massive education and distribution of birth-control devices; limiting families to two children. The problem is education, especially in underdeveloped countries, but also, in a slightly different sense, in the West. Religious and emotional prejudice are the product of centuries of cultural development. The prospect of having to transform the thinking of a significant minority of the people in American society alone is not pleasant — but the alternative is incomprehensible. In view of this, the Pope's recent decision on birth control is a disaster to the prestige of the Catholic Church and a disservice to mankind.

I'm really bugged about this. The crisis may not come in our lifetime, but in the next century, unless something is done, the use of nuclear weapons *will become* a psychological inevitability. Ten billion people is the limit.

Love and peace,
Tim

Saturday, 2nd November, 1968

Dear all —

. . . As I've indicated, the medical business has been brisk recently. I've adapted to the seven hours of sleep I get every night — which would be nothing if I were in school, but in the unstimulating environment of prison it is no mean feat. I'm eating fairly well, though I don't gain any weight — it must be nervous energy that dissipates it, for I don't get enough exercise. Fall is here now, the leaves are turning, and it's become too cold for tennis.

Johnson has finally halted the bombing of North Vietnam — at least a symbolic move, though people are still being killed in the South. If prayer can be thought of merely as an expression of deep subjective longing, and not as an indication of belief in God or as a realistic means of achieving desires, then I pray fervently that the bombing halt leads to peace.

Love and peace,
Tim

Wednesday, 13th November, 1968

Darling Toni —

. . . consider the possibility of a sincere fascist — not just a possibility, but a very probable potentiality. Or consider a person who sincerely believes that some people are "naturally" suited to a condition of slavery — I accept the sincerity of the sentiment and still reject it totally. (The sentiment, that is.) But in these times, in this society, very few people argue explicitly for slavery or for fascism; when their rage or reason point implicitly in either of these directions, they are either unaware of the implications or simply don't care, so strong is their visceral rejection of the tumult of change. So we must consider certain sentiments which are closer to home: for instance, that war is necessary, or that social and political inequalities must be accepted as part of the great scheme of affairs.

A person who believes sincerely that war is inevitable, necessary, and therefore justifiable will usually give one or more of the following reasons: We must defend the honor of our country. We must defend freedom against the evil aggressor. We must not allow communism to expand (this view is a little more sophisticated and politically conscious than the one before it). War is unavoidable in the present order of things and we must go along with it or perish in it. I won't go into the merits, fallacies, and implications of these views right now. The point is that these sentiments are prevalent in our society; they are, all of them, acceptable in the context of our society's mores — just as the ideas of Nordic superiority and Germanic empire were acceptable to most Germans under the Nazi regime, or as slavery was acceptable to most of the people in the Confederate States before the Civil War, including, perhaps, the slaves themselves. (I think you will find that there were about as many black slaves in the South actually clamoring for freedom as there were white abolitionists — in other words, not a great many.) Speaking of the Civil War, it is interesting to note that Robert E. Lee did not feel that he was fighting for the preservation of slavery so much as for the honor of his home state — and only indirectly for the principle of states' rights.

The question of political and social equality has a slightly different hue. While the United States is constitutionally committed to the use of force to "defend its sovereignty" and fulfill its treaty obligations, the constitutional rejection of political inequality is absolute (or has become absolute since the enfranchisement of women and black people.) The difference is also reflected, I think, in the attitudes of many Americans: whereas social injustice is inevitable, it is always wrong, while war is necessary and can be good. In the case of political and social inequality, the issue is only exceptionally one of justice per se; more usually the attitude is, "sure, everybody deserves a fair shake," but things like this take time. On the other hand, it is true that many people simply reject the problem in all its complexity: They're better off than they ever were, and some of *them* are better off than we are; so what right have *they* to raise such a big fuss? In this reasoning, as in the reasoning about war, the implicit justification is that you can't change the way things are without raising more problems than you solve. Also, of course, the idea that change must be moderate and slow is rigidly ingrained in the American character, to the extent that too often people concentrate exclusively on the question of the pace and means of change and ignore the essential issue of what it is that needs to be changed. Just try to get a liberal white American to discuss the problem of achieving social justice; he will almost invariably try to turn the conversation to constitutional process, legislation, courts, education, "reform." It is one great shortcoming of the liberal point of view that it seems to assume that one can achieve an end by ignoring it totally while becoming obsessed with the means to achieve it. The fact is that there is no guarantee that legislation or judicial decisions will be effective in themselves or that they will automatically lead to betterment. Obsession with ends, to the exclusion of any consideration of means, is certainly no way to go about the matter; but the "due process" people have reduced the entire problem to a kind of game in which it matters not that you win or lose, but do you obey the rules. Whether we win or lose not

only matters, it is absolutely the most vital question of the day.
I've got off the subject. I think. Yes. Way off. . . . On the one
hand we can divide up our perceptive and evaluative faculties
and say, "Well, I agree with what you say but not with the way
you say it." Or, "Your point is well taken but your tactics are
abominable." But in any case, how does one really feel? What is
the real issue? Where does one draw the line? Whenever a person chooses an alternative, he places himself in an ambiguous
situation: he cannot claim that he is absolutely right, for that
is unfashionable; but he must defend his choice as the best
alternative he could find and must be committed to it as though
it were absolutely right, because only then does the alternative
stand a chance of becoming right. It is never the vision which
fails, never the glorious possibility which is inadequate; always
it is shortness of will, an implacability of circumstance. Ah, the
world is continually failing our dreams. . . .

T.

16th November, 1968

Darling —
. . . Hypocrisy is never so terrible as when it becomes fixed in
an over-arching order, beyond any individual's life-style, engulf-
ing and stifling the life-styles of many individuals. And that's
part of what prison is: structured, disciplined hypocrisy. Lies
constitute the norm — only extraordinarily are sporadic attempts
at honesty made. And when honesty is attempted, it is perverted
by the unfairness of the odds. There is no prison official here
whom I can approach on a level of personal concern or candor;
the fact that I am a prisoner and he is the guard prohibits that.
There is no sharing except in the most superficial and pointless
way. There is no caring which is not somehow invariably sub-
verted by institutional considerations. We are all prisoners of
the system; our freedom gone, we are powerless to relate to one
another as persons. We are dominated by our roles so totally
and insidiously that the occasional spark of real rapport is corrupt beyond meaning. Every evidence of human warmth is a

mockery, a futile hypocrisy. How can I possibly relate to someone who would shoot me if I should try to gain my freedom? I do not have that freedom. My good humor and cooperation are feeble pretenses. Ultimately, my guards and I meet on uneven ground. It is not we who meet but our roles. Prisoner and guard.

To be actively human is not only desperately difficult under these conditions — it is the only hope. I cannot give that up. . . .

T.

Sunday, 17th November, 1968

Toni darling —

I started reading Erich Fromm's *The Art of Loving*. You ought to read it. Fromm's philosophy of life is almost exactly what I was brought up on by my parents and is very close to my own conception of what Tim and Toni are all about . . . is all about. Fromm has thought it out a lot more thoroughly and comprehensively than I have, so you ought to read him if I sometimes confuse you. The only problem I have with Fromm in this particular book is that his tone tends toward evangelism and his arguments toward oversimplification — but, as Fromm himself says, in love, the art of life, only theory can be discussed; the practice is what counts and it is entirely existential. It sounds trite, Toni, but it's true that nothing worthwhile comes easily; it has to be achieved by, in Fromm's words, "humility, courage, faith and discipline." All these words have an unfortunate connotation of grimness; but to think that life is a field of roses, that the world is a garden of Eden, is far more grim and delusional. Fromm explains it all very well. He only is capable of joy who is also capable of misery. I love you joyfully.

I read this weekend a little booklet on Kennedy's (John) assassination published by *Ramparts*. Even allowing for the anti-establishment slant of the editors, I am persuaded that the Warren Commission's Report is at best a fumbling cover-up. Too much is unexplained; too much evidence is suppressed; too many mistakes were made by those investigating. I am doubtful of the crystal clarity of Garrison's motives in conducting an independent investigation of the assassination, and don't like to posit conspiracy without firm evidence; I do think, though, that especially in something with such a wide and deep impact on history, truth needs to be served above all, and truth has not been served by the official investigation. I doubt that any reasonable court of law would have found Oswald guilty with the evidence on which the Commission based its decision. Oswald was probably not alone; the bullets he fired may not have even been responsible for Kennedy's death. Whatever the actual case, the point is that the evidence was too contradictory and inconclusive to be considered adequate.

T.

Sunday, 24th November

Darling —

There is one state worse than being alone and lonely; that is being lonely but not alone — lonely in a crowd of strangers. Camus knew what I mean, though I mean it not so radically or universally as Camus did. I am temporarily separated from my self, from you, from us — I am the stranger. And though I am not less than myself in this isolation, neither am I fully what I am without you. It is all very well and true to say that because I love you I am therefore better able to love and understand others — rather, our love determines the way in which I learn to love and understand others — still, our separation is not normal or a happy situation, and I am unhappy without you and cannot avoid letting my unhappiness affect my relationships with others. So it goes. It's all or nothing — just as I cannot take only the happiness in our love, so I cannot give only the happiness which I feel. The misery of our separation is eminently present for me, and so it is for everyone who knows me. I cannot distill it out to make myself easier to get along with — I am fractured enough as it is. I love you. Toni. Toni. Toni.

Everything is in a continual state of falling apart. I patch

122

my daily routine together with hope and resignation, no longer expecting to make the vessel seaworthy but only to keep it afloat in its purgatorial dry dock. I miss you so.

T.

Sunday, 1st December, 1968

Darling —

Some commission has just come out with a report on the police-demonstrator confrontation in Chicago last August. The report called the whole thing a "police riot." My feelings about the whole affair are extremely complicated. I think that I more or less expected the police to behave as they did, and I am more upset by the rudeness and pointless tantrums of the demonstrators than I am by the beatings. Maybe I expect more of the demonstrators than I do of the police. Discipline seems to be out of favor at the moment, but disciplined self-restraint is absolutely essential to any scenario of confrontation. I am sure that many of the demonstrators who taunted the police and threw bottles and stones at them were acting on the very same principle as the pervert on a crowded subway: that anonymity excuses individual responsibility. That is deplorable. I think I'm almost overreacting: it's disgusting. Even though, for practical reasons, we cannot always treat one another as we relate to our most intimate friends, nothing is served by carrying our public relationships to the opposite extreme. Even if we consciously believed that the police embody an overwhelming evil — in this case, fascism — a violent, crisis-oriented response is not only unrealistic and reprehensible tactically, but it furthermore demeans us morally by giving our cause the same essential legitimization (i.e., supremacy through violence) which we so despise in the evil that we are protesting. As some astute commentator has put it, I would no more like to be ruled by a police-state headed by Mark Rudd than I would by one headed by Mayor Daley. (Or something to that effect.)

T.

Thursday, 12th December, 1968

Darling —

I have recently come to realize that the difference between "desires" and "needs" is of critical philosophical significance. What a person needs constitutes the minimum demands and satisfactions necessary to psychic and physical health; they are those things withdrawal or attenuation of which would lead to death, whether physical or psychological. Beyond these "needs," however, are desires or strivings which constitute the human potentiality for creativity, fulfillment, self-realization. Needs are very general and are fulfilled very generally. Desires, on the other hand, while they have a common existential source in all men, are expressed and seek fulfillment only in unique and specific relationships. Like Toni and Tim. If our love were a result merely of mutual need, we'd be in a bad way. But one could almost say that our mutual need is a result of love that is very good and rich with potential. Contrary to what some may say, a relationship is not necessarily good because it satisfies needs — that is the absolute minimum that it should do, and such a relationship is merely necessary. The quality of a relationship is defined by the extent to which it takes its meaning from desires and positive strivings. If I say I need you, Toni, that is to say almost nothing. When I say I desire you or love you, that is what really counts.

T.

Epilogue

I WAS PAROLED from prison in the middle of March, 1969. By luck, the spring term at Earlham College began a week after I got out of prison, so I started right back to school after spending a week with my family. It was a breathless week, filled with all the activity and frustration of trying to find my way in the free world again. Everybody had changed a little — I more than others, I think — and it's a rare relationship that can survive so long a separation intact. In a way I felt as though I was starting from scratch, but heavily encumbered by the baggage of the past. Memories and dreams — especially memories and dreams nursed and cultivated in prison — are invariably undone by reality.

People ask me how it feels to be free again. It's no blinding flash of light or euphoric revelation. Being free again consists mostly of very simple things like walking down a street after midnight, lying in the sun on a Saturday afternoon, going to a movie and eating popcorn, smiling at strangers and little children (who are never strangers), shopping for groceries, browsing in bookstores. Being free is very simple; I wish I'd known about it before.

And, of course, people ask me, "Would you do it all over again?" I guess what they mean is "Was the whole thing worthwhile?" That is not a simple question to answer. I can't persuade myself that I accomplished any positive good by going to prison; I didn't help anybody particularly; I didn't do anything positive to make the world a better place to live in. I went to prison because I had to, for the sake of my own integrity. Selfish, perhaps, but how could I have given up something so essential to what I am and still have called my life my own? If I hadn't taken a stand to define myself by saying "No" to what I felt was an indefensible injustice, I would no longer have had any right to trust my own convictions; I would no longer have been what I knew I should be, and whatever I might have been able to do for or give to others would have been dishonest. So, at most I have to say that I cannot judge whether the whole experience was worthwhile — simply because it was so absolutely necessary. An imperative brooks no such judgments.

It's sad, in a way, that the whole thing had to happen. There is something wrong with any society which has to coerce its members into what is defined as socially useful behavior, because that means that there is some important difference between the society and its members, between the nation and the people. Is that really what life is all about? Are we all just raw material for the factory of the national interest? Who is to determine what kind of life is good for me, for anybody? Whose freedom is the state protecting? The people's? Perhaps so, except that I am part of the people, and the state saw fit to violate my freedom. Who are the people? You and I are the people. There is no such thing as the people except as "the people" includes you and me; and there is no such thing as the freedom of the people unless it means your freedom and mine. I had to do what I did because I am not alone; you and I are the people; we are what society is all about; it is our interest that the state is supposed to serve and not the other way around.

I don't think I have tried to avoid responsibility. I have tried, instead, to affirm the real responsibility of each individual for his own actions and for his fellow human beings. No, I have not avoided responsibility; I have refused to give it up. The responsibility rests with you and me, just as the freedom does. There is no true freedom without responsibility, no true responsibility without freedom.

I am back at school now. The war in Vietnam goes on; people are starving in Biafra; sabers are being rattled in the Middle East; the Czechs have lost their freedom and are clinging desperately to their responsibility; three hundred years of oppression in America is bringing its toll of hatred and racism — Black and White. Sometimes I wonder what I'm doing here.

Peace.

4 May, 1969

TIMOTHY ZIMMER